Coaching Models: A Cultural Perspective

Coaching Models: A Cultural Perspective encourages and assists students and practitioners of business coaching to develop and apply their own coaching models. The entire field of coaching will benefit from having coaches who use their models to continually improve their practice.

The first part of this book presents the model development process by looking at the relationship among culture, beliefs, and behavior in the coaching context. It explains the importance of identifying cultural factors that influence the way coaches approach coaching interactions, and their coaching models.

The second part provides coaches with information and strategies for developing personalized coaching models, applying them to specific contexts, and reflecting on their interactions to refine their core coaching practices.

The third part describes the evolution of the author's own coaching model—the Performance Coaching Model—and illustrates how one coach incorporates unique perspectives and sets of skills, knowledge, and experience in her coaching practice.

Diane Lennard, Ph.D., is a coach and Clinical Associate Professor of Management Communication at New York University Stern School of Business. In her course, Foundations of Business Coaching, full-time and part-time MBAs, Executive MBAs, and other graduate students develop, apply, and present their own coaching models. In addition to coaching students, faculty, and administrators at NYU, she coaches business executives, consultants, and other professionals.

Coaching Models:
A Cultural Perspective

A Guide to Model Development for Practitioners and Students of Coaching

Diane Lennard

Routledge
Taylor & Francis Group

NEW YORK AND LONDON

First published 2010
by Routledge
270 Madison Avenue, New York, NY 10016

Simultaneously published in the UK
by Routledge
2 Park Square, Milton Park, Abingdon, Oxon OX14 4RN

Routledge is an imprint of the Taylor & Francis Group, an informa business

© 2010 Taylor & Francis

Typeset in Minion by
RefineCatch Limited, Bungay, Suffolk
Printed and bound in the United States of America on acid-free paper by
Walsworth Publishing Company, Marceline, MO

Library of Congress Cataloging-in-Publication Data
Lennard, Diane, 1953–
    Coaching models : a cultural perspective. A guide to model development
    for practitioners and students of coaching / Diane Lennard.
        p. cm.
        [etc.]
    1. Employees—Coaching of.   2. Executive coaching.   3. Employees—
    Coaching of—Case studies.   4. Executive coaching—Case studies.
    I. Title.
    HF5549.5.C53L53 2010
    658.3′124—dc22   2009040394

ISBN10: 0–415–80213–X (hbk)
ISBN10: 0–415–80214–8 (pbk)
ISBN10: 0–203–87635–0 (ebk)

ISBN13: 978–0–415–80213–0 (hbk)
ISBN13: 978–0–415–80214–7 (pbk)
ISBN13: 978–0–203–87635–0 (ebk)

CONTENTS

ACKNOWLEDGEMENTS

I want to acknowledge the graduate students in my courses who have challenged my thinking and have helped me to clarify my ideas about coaching models. I am grateful to the deans and administrators at the NYU Stern School of Business who have supported my work. I am indebted to Tita Beal for her encouragement and guidance throughout the writing process. I want to thank Mandy Gardner, Bethene LeMahieu, and Shana Carroll for reviewing a complete draft of the book and giving me insightful feedback that significantly influenced the direction of the book. I also want to thank the coaches who shared their models with me, including Suzanne Aptman, Maria Arnone, Deepa Awal, Rachel Ciporen, Phyllis Haynes, Eric Kruger, Carol Langrehr, Eric Marcus, Harriett Simon Salinger, Donna Steinhorn, and Jean Sun Shaw. I acknowledge with appreciation the support of Robert Anderson, Kara Blackburn, Basma Ibrahim DeVries, Nancy Hale, Barbara Kappler, Alice Kolb, Mack Lipkin, Susan Meyer, Adair Nagata, Dianne Nersesian, Dan Newby, Stephanie Nickerson, Tony Pearson, Diane Simpson, and Susan Stehlik. I also acknowledge all of my clients who have contributed to the development of my coaching practice. I dedicate this book to Davina Lennard, who helped with the graphics, and Zia Lennard with gratitude for their generous support and encouragement.

PREFACE

This book is about you, the coach. It is about your purpose for coaching, your process, and your unique contribution to the field of coaching. It's about developing and refining your own model of coaching, whether you are a new or experienced practitioner, or a manager who coaches employees.

In this book, you review coaching concepts and theories that are fundamental to understanding coaching models. Then you explore strategies for developing personalized coaching models. Reflective activities heighten your awareness of the influences on your approach to coaching and personal strengths you can incorporate into your model. Case examples demonstrate how coaches can develop a personalized model that turns their experiences, skills, and interests into authentic strategies to support the people they coach.

The coach is an integral part of the coaching process, as important as the client yet often overlooked. While an understanding of the needs of clients and employees is essential, equally important is the need to reflect on the personal values, strengths, and paradigms that inform your approach to coaching. Just as no two clients are alike, no two coaches or coaching approaches are exactly the same.

Effective coaching means bringing yourself into the process. The more you understand what matters to you about the coaching process and recognize what you uniquely bring to your practice, the better you can serve the needs of the people you coach. It might seem strange to focus on yourself when executive and management coaching is principally about the goals and needs of clients and employees. But, in fact, self-reflection and insights gained about your method and approach to coaching will make you a far more effective coach.

Rather than relying on intuition or someone else's method, you can develop and apply a coaching model that incorporates your own values, strengths, and unique perspectives. When you have a uniquely tailored process, you bring authenticity to coaching interactions and align yourself with people you coach, even if they have very different ways of seeing the world or conflicting cultural values.

BACKGROUND

During my career, I have developed my own personalized approach to coaching and have been struck by the number and breadth of others' unique approaches to coaching. One approach may be based in systems theory, another may draw on cognitive or behavioral theory, and still others may be based on principles of psychoanalysis. The journey of writing this book on the development of a coaching model began when I listened to coaches and managers describe their diverse practices and respond to descriptions of my own coaching practice. Coaches were interested in the model I had developed, one that I currently apply to my work in a university and the corporate environment; I was equally intrigued by the range of perspectives that inform the emerging field of business coaching.

I began to explore personalized coaching models in a graduate-level course on the foundations of business coaching that I teach at New York University's Leonard N. Stern School of Business. To give students a better understanding of the coaching process, to encourage them to "own" the process, and to provide ways to continually improve their coaching effectiveness, I ask them to develop their own coaching models. The results have been astounding. Some examples of the models constructed by these MBA students include:

- A student with an engineering background used a bridge ("over troubled waters") metaphor. He framed communication techniques as suspension cables, past experiences and relevant beliefs of both coach and client as smaller cables stitching the roadway to the suspension, and commitment to the goal as girders of the bridge.
- Another student, who worked as a project manager responsible for implementing technology systems, created a framework for empowerment coaching informed by Ken Blanchard's situational leadership model. The five-step coaching process

empowers his team to make decisions and solve problems on their own.

- A high achiever, studying in NYU's law and business joint degree program, developed an executive coaching model specifically tailored to fellow high achievers. To address the target audience's strong need for autonomy, she emphasized client self-assessment, self-management, and self-reflection.

Every model reflected the individual coach's background, style, and unique perspectives. These students of coaching not only developed unique approaches, they created invaluable tools for critical reflection on their coaching practice.

A coaching model helps the practitioner understand the coaching experience and, by extension, does the same for the person being coached. In addition, a coaching model serves as a tool for new and experienced coaches to sustain a commitment to continuous learning. When coaches continue to reflect on their models, they continue to learn. Continuous learning is crucial to high quality performance as a coach. In this book, a chapter on the work of learning theorists brings together research findings on how you—and the people you coach— can learn, change, and improve performance.

Improvement in coaching effectiveness by one coach leads to improvement in the field of coaching as a whole and to positive results for the people being coached. In short, the process of coaching model development can lead to high quality coaching, raising the bar for both the training of coaches, and the practice of coaching.

This book encourages and assists students of coaching, professional coach practitioners, and managers to develop or refine then apply their own coaching models. Not only will coaches—and their clients or employees—benefit from a personalized model, but the entire field of coaching will also benefit from having coaches who use their models to learn and continually improve their practice.

OVERVIEW

Part I of *Coaching Models: A Cultural Perspective* introduces an approach to coaching model development. Chapter 1 presents five basic ideas that are fundamental to understanding coaching models. I describe several coaching models to illustrate the diverse ways in which practitioners approach coaching. Chapter 2 provides an overview of theories that lay the foundation for coaching model development. I explain select theories from three domains of adult education that are most relevant and may be most useful to coaches who are developing their models. Chapter 3 builds on the learning theories by providing theory-based guidelines for the process of developing a personalized coaching model. I include a series of questions for stimulating coaches to think about their own experiences and perspectives, as well as the relationship among culture, beliefs, and behavior in a coaching context. I encourage coaches to identify cultural and individual factors that influence how they approach coaching interactions, as well as their repertoire of skills, preferred methods and tools, and views about the desired outcomes of coaching.

Part II of *Coaching Models: A Cultural Perspective* provides information and practical strategies for developing personalized coaching models. Chapter 4 describes functions and characteristics of useful coaching models. I include some practitioners' coaching models as examples of personalization. Chapter 5 presents strategies and reflective activities to assist coaches in identifying and selecting components for their coaching models. I emphasize the importance of making explicit the nature of their approach to coaching and suggest a process for model development.

Part III of *Coaching Models: A Cultural Perspective* illustrates how one coach developed and applies a personalized coaching model. Chapter 6 describes the evolution of my coaching model—the Performance Coaching Model. I present pertinent information about my background, beliefs, and behaviors in a coaching context, as an example of how a coach can incorporate unique perspectives and sets of skills, knowledge, and experience into a coaching practice. Chapter 7 discusses various applications of the Performance Coaching Model. I suggest that coaches and managers use their own models as tools for continual learning, reflecting on their interactions, and ways to apply their coaching models.

Diane Lennard
New York, NY

Part I
The Foundation

1

INTRODUCTION TO COACHING MODEL DEVELOPMENT

There is now an abundance of literature on coaching as a way to facilitate the learning and performance of clients, but little has been written about facilitating the learning and performance of coaches. Many of the books and articles describe effective coaching models but few recommend that coaches develop their own approach to coaching, based on their unique combination of strengths.

Whereas *coaching* helps clients, *coaching models* help coaches. *Coaching* is a dynamic interaction that facilitates the learning, development, and performance of the person being coached. *Coaching models* facilitate the learning, development, and performance of coaches.

This chapter presents five basic ideas that are fundamental to understanding coaching models and their development:

1. Coaching models are tools for coaches.
2. Cultural factors influence coaching beliefs and practices.
3. There is no one right way to coach.
4. Coaches learn and coaching models evolve.
5. Start from where you are.

1. COACHING MODELS ARE TOOLS FOR COACHES

What is a *model*? A model is an intellectual device that highlights the key elements of a process and their interrelationships. It can be visual or verbal. A model includes whatever elements the developer considered most essential and eliminates others. It does not replicate every detail of a process, event, or phenomenon.

In this book, a *coaching model* refers to a general guide or a framework of ideas for understanding and navigating an approach to coaching. Coaching models help practitioners and students of coaching think about and understand the process of coaching. Coaches can use their model to generate interesting questions for reflection on coaching effectiveness, then to guide improvements.

The use of a model can lead to greater insight and understanding, as well as new ways of thinking about the structure and process of coaching. A model simplifies and clarifies the complexities of coaching. Rather than ignore the complexity of the coaching process, coaches can use a model to focus on essential factors and manage the complexity. Although individual models may differ, they focus on what is fundamental to coaching and give coherence to the underlying structure of the coaching process.

As a conceptual tool, the coaching model facilitates the process of inquiry that is crucial to ongoing learning about coaching effectiveness. Because a model clarifies the big picture and highlights specific elements of coaching, you can use your model as a springboard for such questions as: What are the boundaries of coaching? What core practices am I using and why? Where do I need to put more attention? To answer questions like these, reflection is required. Your responses may change as you reflect on your coaching process, assess your effectiveness, and evaluate your practice. In fact, more than likely, they will. Therefore, keep in mind that your coaching model is a work in progress. You can refine and modify it over time.

It is critically important for experienced and new coach practitioners to develop their own unique frameworks for thinking about the structure and process of coaching. Why would you invest the time to do this? Bottom line: when you develop your own clearly articulated, critically evaluated coaching model, you give yourself a tool that can guide your actions, place needed boundaries around your coaching practice, and facilitate planning for improved coaching effectiveness.

2. CULTURAL FACTORS INFLUENCE COACHING BELIEFS AND PRACTICES

Individual perspectives influence each practitioner's approach to coaching and those perspectives are significantly influenced by culture. Often the term *culture* is used to refer only to nationality, but all people (coaches and those who are coached) have their own *individual* cultural orientation. The term *individual cultural orientation* refers to your sense of identity and the way you see the world as reflected in the complex interplay of your values, attitudes, and behavior. It informs your approach to coaching, consciously or not. Therefore, a focus on your individual cultural orientation becomes an integral part of developing your own coaching model.

For the purposes of this book, a basic definition of culture advanced by Edgar Schein in his book *Organizational Culture and Leadership* will be used:

> Culture is "a pattern of shared basic assumptions that was learned by a group as it solved its problems of external adaptation and internal integration, that has worked well enough to be considered valid and, therefore, to be taught to new members as the correct way to perceive, think, and feel in relation to those problems" (2004, 17).

By recognizing that humans are cultural beings, each with complex cultural identities, coaches increase their ability to relate to others and to identify influences on their own ways of thinking and acting in coaching situations.

Marshall Singer, who researched patterns of perception and identity, noted that each person has a unique set of group identities and experiences; each person is culturally unique. He points out that every identity group has a culture of its own, and every individual is a part of many different identity groups and cultures simultaneously. He stated that "because no person is a part of all and only the same groups as anyone else and because each person ranks the attitudes, values, and beliefs of the groups to which he or she belongs differently, which is what culture is all about, *each individual must be considered to be culturally unique*" (Singer 1998, xiii). No two individuals share the exact same group memberships or give the same importance to the group memberships they share. Consider the various groups that people belong to and how these may influence their cultural orientation—an industry, a discipline, an organization, a family of origin, a country of origin, educational institutions, a gender, a socioeconomic class, an age group, a language, a philosophy.

The practice of coaching is immeasurably strengthened when coaches develop and work with a coaching model that takes into account their individual cultural orientation—their unique set of experiences and perspectives—and the cultural context of the choices they make. While you cannot be completely free from your cultural conditioning, you can remain flexible and open to responding, adapting, and changing when you communicate with a culturally different person.

By acknowledging and appreciating this, you can partner more effectively with the people you coach and not impose your own beliefs and values.

To develop your model, you need to recognize and understand your individual cultural orientation. The greater your awareness of personal style, behavioral tendencies, and hot buttons, the better you can manage these influences, and not impede the success of the coaching interaction. Equally important is your awareness of your own individual cultural identity, derived from membership in groups that have informed your values, beliefs, and behaviors. Your core values influence the way you see the world. They affect your attitudes towards behaviors you consider most appropriate and effective in each situation. Your unique set of perspectives and experiences influence the way you approach your coaching process and practice.

The renowned anthropologist Edward T. Hall states that "there is not one aspect of human life that is not touched and altered by culture" (1976, 16). Becoming aware of the cultural influences on your own approach to coaching, the unique perspectives as well as the skills you bring to your practice, requires self-reflection. This might include such questions as: What core values and beliefs drive your behavior in a coaching context? What draws you to coaching? What are your goals for coaching? What skills do you want to apply to coaching interactions? What are your areas of expertise, capabilities, and strengths? What are your preferred coaching methods and tools? What are the underlying principles of your coaching approach and the ethical guidelines that matter to you?

Consider also how your views of coaching may be inspired and informed by philosophical or theoretical frameworks from other disciplines. For example, a coach who values scientific research and development may view coaching as a process of helping people to develop a hypothesis about what to do, then test it out and take action based on evidence; a coach who has an interest in botany may frame coaching as a process of seeding and nurturing clients' growth. Depending on their individual view of the world, each coach may position the coaching model in terms of a preferred paradigm or a guiding metaphor—research, botany or whatever inspires and informs the coach.

Coaching models have personal meaning and resonate with the coaches who develop them. They incorporate the coach's views about people, learning, performance, and organizations. Personalized coaching models may differ, but they share a dynamic structure: a heightened awareness of the coach's own unique viewpoints, values, and preferences. As a result, the coach is more likely to master one of the key competencies of effective coaching: ability to recognize and respect the different viewpoints, values, and perspectives of the people they coach.

3. THERE IS NO ONE RIGHT WAY TO COACH

Just as all coaches have their own individual cultural orientation, they also have skills and areas of expertise that influence their coaching practice. Some coaches are line managers who have moved up the ranks of an organization. Some are practitioners with a background in psychology or counseling. Many draw on years of professional experience in a range of interrelated fields: organizational development, management consulting, training and development, sports, health, education, linguistics, human resources, business strategy; and in my case, marketing, education, and theatre. When developing a coaching model, experienced coaches as well as students of coaching are encouraged to think about the knowledge and skills they have acquired from various disciplines, and how they might integrate them into their approach. Each coach's cultural orientation, personal experiences, and preferred theories and practices matter.

There is no one, universally accepted coaching approach. Nor is there any reason to refrain from using and adapting a multiplicity of approaches. In fact, by examining coaching from a variety of angles and perspectives, you will be better able to distinguish the essential elements of your own coaching process and practice, including the related skills and competencies. Your approach will invariably build on your own experience and the principles and practices of others in coaching and related fields.

To begin to think about developing your personalized coaching model, you may find it helpful to examine the different ways that practitioners approach coaching. Consider the following examples of coaching models:

Timothy Gallwey's Inner Game Model

Timothy Gallwey attended Harvard, was captain of its tennis team, and developed the "Inner Game" model of coaching with origins in sports. Drawing on his experience teaching tennis, he developed a unique approach to unlocking people's potential and helping them become better learners and performers. Gallwey realized his tennis students were incorporating his instructions as "command and control" self-dialogue. Their internal dialogue and negative thinking were interfering, rather than enhancing, performance and learning.

To change this, Gallwey developed ways to focus the mind of the players on something other than hitting the ball back. He asked them to watch the seams of the ball as it spins, or say the word "bounce" out loud the moment the ball hits the court and the word "hit" the moment the ball makes contact with the racket. He also gave players a strategy of asking themselves descriptive, non-judgmental questions (e.g. "How high is the tennis ball as it passes over the net? Which way is the ball spinning as it comes toward you?"). This mental conversation eliminates the interference of unhelpful beliefs (self-talk), generates non-judgmental awareness, and focuses attention. The result was better performance, learning, and enjoyment of the process. Gallwey created a formula to describe his approach:

Performance = potential – interference (2001, 17).

For more than 20 years, Gallwey has applied the "Inner Game" model to business situations. The model has been used to help corporations manage change and develop leaders. It also helps individuals work more effectively in teams.

John Whitmore's GROW Model

John Whitmore developed his model after training with Gallwey and later co-leading the Inner Tennis, Inner Skiing, and Inner Golf holidays with Gallwey. Building on Gallwey's success with athletes, Whitmore created his own model geared specifically to business professionals. His "GROW" model is based on a structured series of open-ended questions, similar to Gallwey's, to raise professionals' awareness of what is happening and what they are experiencing. The questions also heighten their sense of responsibility for their thoughts and actions. The model establishes, examines, and explores:

Goals
Reality of the current situation
Options or action strategies to accomplish the goals
Will or what the client will do.

In sports and in business, Whitmore believes effective coaching maximizes people's performance by helping them learn—as opposed to demanding compliance with the dictates of an external authority. He argues the importance of managers seeing the future potential of their employees, not just their past performance. According to Whitmore, "Coaching is not merely a technique to be wheeled out and rigidly applied in certain prescribed circumstances. It is a way of managing, a way of treating people, a way of thinking, a way of being" (2004, 18).

Whitmore's GROW framework for structuring a coaching session has been used and adapted by many coach practitioners.

Mary Beth O'Neill's Systems Approach to Executive Coaching

Gallwey and Whitmore used personal experience to inform their coaching models. Theoretical frameworks and practices from a wide range of disciplines can also be applied to coaching interactions. Executive coach Mary Beth O'Neill grounds her coaching approach in systems theory and action research, with an orientation to inquiry used in the organizational development field. Her coaching interactions focus on business results and issues related to the system of interrelationships in an organization that influence and are influenced by the client. For O'Neill, "The essence of coaching is helping leaders get unstuck from their dilemmas and assisting them in transferring their learning into results for the organization" (2000, xiii). Using the phases of the action research model, she created a four-phased coaching process.

1. **Phase 1, Contracting**: Joining with the executive; becoming familiar with the executive's challenge; giving immediate feedback; establishing a contract; and encouraging the executive to set measurable goals.
2. **Phase 2, Action planning**: Identifying a specific plan of action, including the actions of the executive; addressing organizational and role alignment issues; and planning for resistance to the executive's actions.
3. **Phase 3, Live action coaching**: Coaching in real time individual or groups of executives as they conduct business activities and implement action plans; and coaching when the executive is in a one-on-one session with another person.
4. **Phase 4, Debriefing**: Evaluating the effectiveness of both the leader being coached and the coach.

Her model combines the phases of action research with a systems perspective.

Bruce Peltier's Psychological Orientation to Executive Coaching

Professor of psychology, licensed psychologist, and executive coach Bruce Peltier focuses on the contribution of the psychoanalytical perspective to executive coaching. He differentiates coaching from therapy, but argues that the two domains of psychotherapy and business coaching have a great deal to offer each other. Peltier defines coaching as:

Someone from outside an organization uses psychological skills to help a person develop into a more effective leader. These skills are applied to specific present-moment work problems in a way that enables this person to incorporate them into his or her permanent management or leadership repertoire (2001, xx).

Peltier believes mental health professionals—therapists, psychologists, counselors, and social workers—can apply their clinical therapeutic experience to the corporate or small business workplace. He also believes that business coaches, who may not have training in psychotherapy, can benefit when they learn about the usefulness and applicability of a wide range of psychological theories that underlie executive coaching practices. For Peltier, coaching is, in fact, a cross-disciplinary practice. He believes that existing knowledge bases can inform each coach's personal framework for understanding and working with clients and employees.

Hunt and Weintraub's Developmental Coaching Model

Often the coaching context will dictate the method used. For instance, James M. Hunt and Joseph R. Weintraub believe managers who coach employees need to internalize a simple framework that can guide their actions and be easily incorporated into their busy daily routines. They conceive of coaching as a way for managers to help their employees develop and learn, describing the ability to coach as a necessary competency for effective managers. "Developmental coaching is a helping relationship between a manager, and most often, his or her employees (though coaching managers may coach others in their organization); its goal is the growth and development of employees" (Hunt and Weintraub 2002, xiii). As part of this developmental process with an employee, the manager:

1. Identifies learning opportunities (coaching moments), then stops the action and starts the coaching dialogue with questions to encourage reflection.
2. Serves as a mirror by observing relevant actions and providing helpful, balanced feedback.
3. Works together with the employee to understand needed change, set a goal for change, and then follow up.

Hunt and Weintraub describe three key requirements for the developmental coaching approach: a manager with a coaching mind-set (focused on the performance of others and on being helpful rather than evaluative); a coach-able learner (motivated to learn and receptive to feedback); a coaching-friendly context (where employees can talk about problems without risk, are expected to solve their own problems, and coaching is continuous).

Zeus and Skiffington's Team Coaching Model

Team coaching requires a different set of practices and can involve either internal or external coaches. Team coaches work with the leader and members of a team to establish their mission, vision, strategy, and operating procedures. Perry Zeus and Suzanne Skiffington, who see the coach as "an expert in the use of behavioral change tools and techniques" (2002, 6), describe a six-step team coaching process that involves working with members of a team over a period of several weeks or months:

Step 1: Meeting with management to determine the appropriateness of team coaching, the organization's needs and resources, the composition of the team; and to clarify logistics of the coaching sessions, including assessing, benchmarking, feedback, and reporting procedures.

Step 2: Individual meetings with each team member to establish rapport, explain coaching roles and agenda, and gather information.

Step 3: First meeting with the team to clarify roles, expectations, and the process; establish confidentiality; agree on objectives for the coaching sessions; and distribute assessments, such as the Team Development Questionnaire, Myers-Briggs Type Indicator (MBTI), or Fundamental Interpersonal Relations Orientation (FIRO).

Step 4: Second meeting with the team to give feedback from the assessments, encourage commitment to team goals and vision, and examine resistance to the proposed goals.

Step 5: Weekly team coaching sessions, each with an established goal and action plan that involve discussions, group exercises, reviews, and feedback.

Step 6: Management feedback about the team's progress given by the coach, including reports on action plans, results, recommendations, and planned follow-up team coaching and individual coaching.

George Renwick's Approach to Coaching Global Executives

Rather than focus on methods or specific tools, George Renwick (2006) created a coaching approach that highlights coaching roles. He describes his approach to coaching global executives in terms of the primary roles he assumes and the possible ways he can contribute to his clients during the coaching interaction process. He is flexible to each coaching situation and each client. He sees himself in different roles at different times with different clients, and adapts himself accordingly. At various times, he sees himself in the role of a:

- *Quiet explorer:* Listening, reflecting back what he hears, asking clarifying questions, and engaging in appreciative inquiry.
- *Creative colleague:* Participating in problem-solving and decision-making by clarifying objectives, jointly generating, and systematically evaluating options.
- *Client-centered tutor:* Providing perspective and insight, as well as identifying, practicing, and refining critical, job-related skills.
- *Seasoned advisor:* Offering practical advice and specific recommendations, or confronting and challenging them in culturally appropriate ways.

Douglas Silsbee's Septet Coaching Model

Another coaching approach that centers around roles coaches play to help people grow is Douglas K. Silsbee's "septet coaching" model (2004). He uses a music metaphor, describing these coaching roles as integrated voices and comparing each to an instrument in a jazz band that knows the exact right time to improvise a creative solo. Each of the following seven voices serves the client in a unique and mutually reinforcing way: *master, partner, investigator, reflector, teacher, guide, and contractor.* Silsbee uses his framework of voices to examine the roles the coach plays in coaching situations.

Travis Kemp's Adventure-Based Coaching Model

Coach practitioners can also develop a coaching approach based on a preferred paradigm, a philosophical, or theoretical framework. For example, Travis Kemp developed an adventure-based coaching approach framed within the metaphoric context of an adventure. It is important to note that not all approaches are suitable for all clients and employees. For example, the adventure-based coaching approach is only suitable for people who are willing to frame their experience in the context of an adventure.

Kemp integrates the experiential learning cycle (Kolb 1984), a process in which the learner makes sense of concrete experiences, with adventure programming: the intentional use of adventure experiences (such as wilderness expeditions or a ropes course) to create learning in individuals and groups. The adventure-based coaching cycle has two phases:

- **Phase 1**: This phase begins with the coach explaining the adventure metaphor and how it applies to the coaching context. It continues with the client choosing a challenge and exploring it so the client has a clearly defined developmental goal that will motivate him or her to action; identifying risks, fears, desirable experiences, and finally, selection of an adventure (such as an executive volunteering at a homeless shelter to develop empathy). It ends with the client and the coach planning the logistics of the adventure.
- **Phase 2**: The second phase involves the client actually participating in the adventure and then convening with the coach to review what happened. From the insights gained, the client chooses and commits to new actions in real-life settings.

The adventure-based coaching process can facilitate the transfer of cognitive and behavioral learning from the adventure experience to similar situations and contexts in the client's real world (Kemp 2006).

Significant similarities exist among these very different structured coaching approaches. Each involves some kind of a relationship established between the coach and the person(s) being coached; a process that has its own logical sequence; an assessment or observation that provides a springboard for dialogue; and a coaching conversation that uses core communication skills. Significant differences also exist among coaching approaches. Some involve internal manager coaches, others external executive coaches. Some focus on individuals, others on groups. Some have a specific theoretical orientation or multiple theoretical perspectives; and some use a metaphor to allow clients to see one aspect of a situation in terms of another, while others do not. It is important to recognize that these examples of coaching approaches incorporate assumptions and methods uniquely suited to the practitioner and tailored for the people they coach. Each approach makes a contribution to the field of coaching. Clearly, there is no one right way to coach.

4. COACHES LEARN AND COACHING MODELS EVOLVE

Whether you are focused on the skills, the development goals, or the personal or professional agenda of the person you coach, you will continually learn. Your coaching model will continually evolve as you reflect on where you are and where you want to go. Again, some fundamental questions: What knowledge and skill sets can you now draw on? What core professional and personal competencies can you now bring to your coaching practice? As you expand your current repertoire of capabilities and integrate new methods and tools into your coaching practice, how is your model evolving? What new knowledge and new skills would you like to develop? What new professional and personal competencies would you like to bring to your practice? Effective coaches recognize and appreciate the need for continual learning.

A coaching model makes your process explicit. It also helps lead you to your own self-development plan. By working with your coaching model and reflecting on actual coaching interactions, you can more readily recognize new coaching skills and behaviors to explore, as well as assumptions to question and qualities to develop in yourself. Once you're attuned to working with your coaching model, you can develop strategies to continue your learning and development as an even more effective coach. As part of this process, you will continue to ask yourself questions related to your work as a coach: What specific actions can I take to develop as a coach? What might I read, reflect on, or do to improve my coaching effectiveness? How can I continue to develop myself while simultaneously coaching others?

5. START FROM WHERE YOU ARE

In this book, you will find an approach to coaching model development that advocates coaching pluralism, that is, a variety of coaching practices to meet the diverse needs of business coaching clients or employees. This approach encourages coaches with different cultural backgrounds, interests, and experiences to develop their own coaching models. You can start from where you are. Whether you are a student of coaching or an experienced coach, you will find information and guidance for the process of developing and refining your own coaching model.

SUMMARY

This chapter has presented five ideas that are fundamental to understanding coaching models and their development:

1. Coaching models are tools for coaches.
2. Cultural factors influence coaching beliefs and practices.

3. There is no one right way to coach.
4. Coaches learn and coaching models evolve.
5. Start from where you are.

Coaching models facilitate the learning, development, and perform-ance of coaches. One key to coaching effectiveness is the coach's ability to learn and make adjustments during coaching interactions, then reflect after each session to learn what improvements are needed going forward. The next chapter includes a review of theories about how adults learn and improve performance.

2

THEORETICAL FOUNDATION
Learning Theory for Coaches

Learning is central to effective coaching and the process of coaching model development. Coaches facilitate the learning process of the people they coach as they identify and plan needed change, and work to achieve goals, making continuous improvements. Coaches, as well as the people they coach, are learners. They learn how each person being coached sees the world and makes meaning of his or her experiences. As coaches develop their own approach to coaching, they engage in learning not only about others, but also about themselves and their coaching process and practice.

It is essential for coaches who are developing a coaching model to understand how adults learn. This chapter presents three domains of adult education that lay the foundation for the development of a coaching model: *adult learning, transformative learning,* and *cross-cultural learning.* Selected learning theories are summarized (see Table 2.1).

The first section of this chapter examines theories of *adult learning* that raise important issues about the learning process, practice, interaction with others, and the environment. Most of the learning theories highlighted in this chapter focus on how adults learn from experience and take ownership of their learning—an essential element of the coaching process. The second section explores theories of *transformative learning* that provide insights into the role of critical reflection, dialogue, and reflective action. The third section presents theories of *cross-cultural learning* that offer concepts and knowledge about cultural differences, value orientations, culture-group membership and its influence on perception and interaction. The chapter ends with a

Table 2.1
Theoretical Foundation for Coaching Model Development

Domains	Theorists	Theories	Themes
1. Adult Learning	Knowles	Andragogy	role of experience
	Argyris and Schon	Action science	role of prior experience
	Lindeman	Adult education	problem-centered orientation
	Brookfield	Adult learning	self-directed learning
	Kolb	Experiential learning	role of current experience
	Lave and Wenger	Situated learning	interpersonal context
	Vygotsky	Social development	cultural context
	Rogers and Maslow	Humanism	learning as a process
2. Transformative Learning	Mezirow	Transformative learning	critical reflection
	Freire	Education for social change	praxis—action and reflection
3. Cross-Cultural Learning	Hofstede	Cultural differences	value dimensions
	Ting-Toomey	Identity negotiation	values and self-concept
	Trompenaars and Hampden-Turner	Intercultural management	cultural dilemmas
	Stewart and Bennett	Intercultural relations	cultural patterns
	Singer	Intercultural communication	cultural uniqueness
	Adler	Cultural identity development	cultural learning
	Langer	Mindful learning	multiple perspectives

discussion of a mindful learning approach that can inform your ways of thinking about engaging in complex and changing situations, expanding awareness, enhancing the capabilities of the people you coach, and your own coaching effectiveness.

ADULT LEARNING

An examination of adult learning theories about the role of experience and awareness can strengthen your ability to identify and select components for your own coaching model. Highlights of the work of adult learning theorists follow—select theories that you can draw on as you develop and refine your coaching model. These include:

- Andragogy and the role of experience—*Malcolm Knowles*
- Action science and the role of prior experience—*Chris Argyris and Donald Schon*
- Adult education and a problem-centered orientation to learning—*Eduard Lindeman*
- Adult learning and self-directed learning—*Stephen Brookfield*
- Experiential learning and the role of current experience—*David Kolb*
- Situated learning and the interpersonal context—*Jean Lave and Etienne Wenger*
- Social development and the cultural context—*Lev Semanovich Vygotsky*
- Humanism and learning as a process—*Carl Rogers and Abraham Maslow*

Andragogy and the Role of Experience
Malcolm Knowles

A central area of focus in adult learning theory involves the role of the learner's experience. The term *andragogy* was coined by Malcolm Shepherd Knowles in 1970 to make the distinction between pedagogic instruction and adult learning principles. One of the core assumptions of andragogy is that experience provides the richest resource for adults' learning. Knowles, as well as many other learning theorists, recognized that adult experiences create habits and assumptions that can shape and limit the learner's openness to new perspectives. The prior experience of learners can have a powerful influence not only on their attitudes toward learning, but on the meanings they give to their lives and the definitions they have for themselves (Knowles, Holton III and Swanson 1998). For coaches, it is important to understand that adult learning is primarily concerned with experience—accumulating it, storing it, and recalling it to interpret new experiences. Just as clients and employees bring their accumulated experiences to coaching situations, coaches bring a wide range of experiences to the coaching model development process. As discussed throughout this book, coaching models draw on the coaches' personal and professional experiences.

Action Science and the Role of Prior Experience
Chris Argyris and Donald Schon

Chris Argyris and Donald Schon investigated the role that prior experience plays in shaping and permitting or preventing new learning. Over the past 20 years, their research has focused on different aspects of human action and the ways in which learning fits or does not fit the learner's prior experience. Much of their work together concentrated on the importance of overcoming resistance to new learning that challenges existing mental schema—the cognitive structures that stem from previous experience and serve as a basis for assimilating new information. Argyris and Schon have written extensively about personal change, professional development, organizational learning, and leadership effectiveness. Individually and together, their work focused on issues that are keys to effective coaching: helping people overcome the tendency to resist new learning; increase interpersonal effectiveness; and make informed action choices in an uncertain and rapidly changing world.

Knowing-in-Action and Reflection-in-Action

Schon's research focused on the nature of professional knowledge, as well as the role of experience in shaping learning, and imagining and realizing alternative practices. He concluded that many professional practitioners perceive professional knowledge as being "mismatched to the changing character of the situations of practice—the complexity, uncertainty, instability, uniqueness, and value conflicts which are increasingly perceived as central to the world of professional practice" (Schon 1983, 14). In his view, developing an appreciation and understanding of the context for professional action is central to effective practice.

Schon conceptualized the development of this understanding as *reflection-in-action*. He described reflection-in-action as an essentially artistic process in which the practitioner makes judgments and exercises skills without an explicitly articulated rationale, but with an intuitive sense of professional correctness, confidence, and accumulated experience. Combining reflection on a new and surprising situation with experimentation and implementation of intuitively chosen practices, the practitioner constructs "a new theory of the unique case" (Schon 1983, 68). Schon advocated a "broader, deeper, and more rigorous" use of reflection-in-action for professional practitioners (1983, 69).

The sequential process of reflection-in-action begins with a situation to which the learner or practitioner spontaneously responds with tacit *knowing-in-action.* Schon described his concept of knowing-in-action as a type of know-how that we exhibit when performing observable physical tasks, such as riding a bicycle or analyzing a balance sheet: "In both cases, the knowing is *in* the action. We know it by our spontaneous, skillful execution of the performance and we are characteristically unable to make it verbally explicit" (1987, 25). When routine responses to a situation produce an unexpected outcome that does not fit into existing categories of knowing-in-action, the surprise gets our attention. This leads to reflection while *in* the action—consciously self-questioning and critically thinking about the assumptions of our knowing-in-action.

Reflection of this type has immediate significance to human action, including coaching, because it leads to experimenting in real time (the present moment) with restructured strategies and new understandings to deal with the newly observed phenomena. New actions may lead to intended results or more surprises that call for more reflection and more experimentation. Reflection-in-action is a single process, rather than a two-part activity of critical reflection and action. It involves learning by doing (practice-based learning), tacit knowing (knowing-in-action), and self-awareness (reflection-in-action).

An adult can reflect while performing an action and as a result discover mental schema that are no longer appropriate, as well as shift to ones that are more appropriate. This insight recognizes the human ability to engage in a situation before having a full understanding of it. Schon explained that the adult learner or practitioner in the process of reflection-in-action makes use of an extensive repertoire of images, metaphors, and theories, allowing for different ways of framing situations:

> When a practitioner makes sense of a situation he perceives to be unique, he *sees* it as something already present in his repertoire. [. . .] The familiar situation functions as a precedent, or a metaphor, or—in Thomas Kuhn's (1977) phrase—an exemplar for the unfamiliar one (Schon 1987, 67).

Schon emphasized that reflecting while performing an action permits inventiveness and creativity in the moment.

Schon's learning theories and insights into the preparation of professionals emphasize creative patterns of action that are useful, legitimate aspects of learning and performance. His approach to education for artistry through reflection-in-action applies to the artistry of everyday life, as well as to professional practice. Such an approach can serve a wide variety of learning situations, including coaching.

Artistry is an exercise of intelligence, a kind of knowing, though different in crucial respects from our standard model of professional knowledge. It is not inherently mysterious; it is rigorous in its own terms; and we can learn a great deal about it—within what limits, we should treat as an open question—by studying the performance of unusually competent performers (Schon 1987, 13).

A pianist and clarinetist who played in jazz and chamber groups, Schon examined the artistry of outstanding practitioners in various disciplines. He believed that artistry is an essential component of professional competence.

Schon's view of reality was constructivist. He saw practitioners constructing situations of practice in order to exercise professional artistry and competence:

In the terrain of professional practice, applied science and research-based technique occupy a critically important though limited territory, bounded on several sides by artistry. There is an art of problem framing, an art of implementation, and an art of improvisation—all necessary to mediate the use in practice of applied science and technique (Schon 1987, 13).

Challenging the premise of technical rationality, Schon offered an alternative epistemology of practice that recognizes professional knowledge embedded in the context shared by a community of practitioners. His concept of reflection-in-action has practical relevance for coaches who continually learn while in action. Coaches can also use their awareness of the value of reflection-in-action as they coach people who are taking actions discussed in coaching sessions.

Double Loop Learning: Bringing Theories of Action into Congruence

Donald Schon worked with Chris Argyris, teaching, consulting, and researching human action from the 1970s to the 1990s. Schon and Argyris integrated the concepts of knowing-in-action, reflection-in-action, and reflective practice into a theory of action that examines reality from the perspective of people as actors. They noted that people have mental maps that determine how they plan, implement, and review their actions. These mental maps guide people's behavior and may be different from the theories they espouse.

Argyris' and Schon's theory of *double loop learning* differentiates "espoused theory" (values that people believe their actions are based on) from "theory-in-use" (values implied by their actions). Double loop learning is the process of bringing the two different "theories of action" into congruence. Learners discover their theories of action, question underlying values and assumptions, invent new meanings, produce and test new actions, and generalize the results. "In single loop learning, we learn to maintain the field of constancy by learning to design actions that satisfy existing governing variables. In double loop learning, we learn to change the field of constancy itself" (Argyris and Schon 1974, 19). By changing the mental maps that provide meaning and organization to previous experience, adult learners allow information to extend beyond the reason it was given. They can imagine alternative ways of thinking and acting. Double loop learning is a theory and a practice of personal change that integrates thought and action.

Argyris and Schon suggested that the key to successful practice in the real world is "developing one's own continuing theory of practice under real-time conditions" (1974, 157). According to the double loop learning model, professionals who are effective in the real world base their practice on valid information, exercise free and informed choice over practice activities, and show an internal commitment to the chosen action while monitoring its implementation. Argyris and Schon believed that the most effective practitioners and learners are successful at double loop learning and reflection-in-action. Effective coach practitioners reflect critically on their underlying assumptions and consider alternatives to their current ways of thinking and acting. They both facilitate and engage in double loop learning and reflection-in-action.

Adult Education and a Problem-Centered Orientation to Learning
Eduard Lindeman

Recognition of the adult's problem-centered and performance-centered orientation to learning is critical to understanding adult learning behavior. Adults are motivated to learn what will help them perform tasks and resolve problems. They also want to become competent at applying new skills and knowledge to real-life situations. "Every adult person finds himself in specific situations with respect to his work, his recreation, his family life, his community life, etc.—situations which call for adjustments. Adult education begins at this point" (Lindeman 1926, 8–9).

In 1926, Eduard C. Lindeman advanced a process of *adult education* in which learners become aware of significant experience, evaluate it, and find accompanying meanings relevant to their everyday lives. According to Lindeman, it is the experience and knowledge of learners that play the primary role in adult education:

> Too much of learning consists of vicarious substitution of some-
> one else's experience and knowledge. Psychology is teaching us,

however, that we learn what we do, and that therefore all genuine education will keep doing and thinking together [. . .] Experience is the adult learner's living textbook (1926, 8–9).

His vision for adult education involved a concern for people's experience and the educational possibilities of everyday life. He laid the foundation for a theory of adult learning that begins with the learner's needs and interests. Lindeman and John Dewey, his friend and colleague, shared a commitment to inquiry as problem-solving, and a belief in the possibilities of education and human action. Their views form a useful foundation for coaching and coaching model development because they emphasize the pragmatic nature of adult learning and the self-determination of adult learners.

Adult Learning and Self-Directed Learning
Stephen Brookfield

Stephen Brookfield, whose main research activities have focused on the nature of *adult learning* and self-directed learning in particular, stated that "adults engage in an educational activity because of some innate desire for developing new skills, acquiring new knowledge, improving already assimilated competencies or sharpening powers of self insight" (1986, 11). Brookfield emphasized the voluntary nature of the adult learner's participation in learning. The motivation for learning is high. Even if prompted by an external circumstance, such as a job loss, the decision to engage actively in learning is the learner's. Participation can easily be withdrawn if a learning activity does not build on experience or meet the learner's needs and concerns.

At the heart of self-initiated, significant learning is the importance of both experience and awareness. Brookfield believed that the learning process must include both practice in applying skills and knowledge, and reflection on actual experiences. He wrote extensively about the importance for adult learners to develop the powers of critical reflection in order to discover the meaning of experience:

The most fully adult form of self-directed learning, however, is one in which critical reflection on the contingent aspects of reality, the exploration of alternative perspectives and meaning systems, and the alteration of personal and social circumstances are all present. The external technical and the internal reflective dimensions of self-directed learning are fused when adults come to appreciate the culturally constructed nature of knowledge and values and when they act on the basis of that appreciation to reinterpret and recreate their personal and social worlds. In such a praxis of thought and action is manifested a fully adult form of self-directed learning (Brookfield 1986, 58–9).

The concept of self-directed learning relates to the role of experience in shaping the adult's orientation to learning. It recognizes both external factors that facilitate learners taking primary responsibility for planning, implementing, and evaluating their own learning experiences, and internal factors that predispose adults to accept responsibility for their learning.

Brookfield and other adult learning theorists discussed in this chapter, such as Lindeman and Knowles, emphasized the concept of self-directed learning. Brookfield suggested that the purpose of learning should be to develop self-directed learning capacity in adults. Lindeman assumed that adults have a need to be self-directing. Knowles conceptualized self-directed learning as personal autonomy: "Autonomy means taking control of the goals and purposes of learning and assuming ownership of learning. This leads to an internal change of consciousness in which the learner sees knowledge as contextual and freely questions what is learned" (1998, 135). Knowles' concept of andragogy assumes that learners see themselves as being personally autonomous and capable of self-direction. According to Knowles, andragogy is a theory of adult learning based on the precepts that adults want to maintain responsibility for their own decisions and lives, and to learn those things that they need to know in order to cope effectively with real-life situations. In one sense, as coaches develop their own personalized coaching models, they are self-directed learners who are taking control of, and responsibility for, their own learning.

Experiential Learning and the Role of Current Experience
David Kolb

David Kolb, an influential proponent of adult learning based in experience, defined *experiential learning* as "the process whereby knowledge is created through transformation of experience" (1984, 38). He believed that content and experience interact and transform each other. Kolb was interested in exploring the learner-centered processes associated with making sense of concrete experiences.

Drawing from the works of John Dewey, Jean Piaget, and Kurt Lewin, he developed the experiential learning model of how people learn from their experience. The four steps in Kolb's experiential learning cycle are:

1. Engaging in real-time experiences: *concrete experience.*
2. Viewing experiences from multiple perspectives: *reflective observations.*

3. Forming concepts that integrate observations into theories: *abstract conceptualization.*
4. Using theories to make decisions and solve problems: *active experimentation.*

Learners participate in concrete learning activities, then reflect, and based on that, formulate ideas while taking others' expert opinions into account. Kolb's model is a useful conceptual framework for designing and planning adult learning experiences. For example, a design for a learning sequence might include a demonstration; small group activities; reflective discussion; and practice sessions. Experiential learning theory is central to understanding how people learn in any context, including in a coaching situation.

Situated Learning and the Interpersonal Context
Jean Lave and Etienne Wenger

Learning is a complex process, often influenced by the context in which it takes place. It follows then that a study of the nature of the adult learning experience must consider the important role that the interpersonal context plays. When learners engage with the world, they construct meaning out of it. Following in the path of Dewey and Piaget, constructivists believe that learners construct knowledge for themselves as they learn. Constructivist theories recognize learning as the construction of meaning—an active, social, contextual process.

Situated learning theory focuses on learning from the experience of participating in daily life, constructing identity and meaning in a social context, and the interplay of knowledge and practice. Jean Lave, a social anthropologist, and Etienne Wenger, Ph.D., a specialist in artificial intelligence, introduced the concept that adult learning involves participation in a community of practice: "A person's intentions to learn are engaged and the meaning of learning is configured through the process of becoming a full participant in a sociocultural practice. This social process includes, indeed it subsumes, the learning of knowledgeable skills" (1991, 29). Situated learning theory recognizes the importance of social interaction, context, and collaboration in the adult learning process.

Lave and Wenger conducted a research study in 1991 that analyzed situated learning among different groups of people, including Yucatec midwives, native tailors, navy quartermasters, and meat cutters. In each case, they found that novices gradually acquired knowledge and skills from experts in the context of everyday activities:

In this there is a concern with identity, with learning to speak, act and improvise in ways that make sense in the community. What is more, and in contrast with learning as internalization, learning as increasing participation in communities of practice concerns the whole person acting in the world (Lave and Wenger, 1991, 49).

The work of Lave and Wenger focused on how knowledge develops in the course of action that is situated in relationships, social roles and situations of active participation in the shared practices of communities. An essential feature of this theory for coaching and coaching model development is that learning occurs naturally in the context of doing the activity and in solving real problems.

Social Development and the Cultural Context
Lev Semanovich Vygotsky

Interaction with other people and the environment also play a role in understanding the nature of the adult learning experience. The primary role of social interaction, a key component of situated learning theory, can also be seen in the theoretical writings of constructivist thinker Lev Semanovich Vygotsky. He believed that the lifelong process of development is dependent on social interaction, and that social learning leads to cognitive development. Vygotsky emphasizes this in his *social development theory* of learning:

> Every function in the child's cultural development appears twice: first, on the social level, and later, on the individual level; first, between people (interpsychological) and then inside the child (intrapsychological). All the higher functions originate as actual relationships between individuals (1978, 57).

Many of Vygotsky's theories focused on the interdependent process of development and the cultural context in which interactions and experiences are shared. His concept that learning requires social interaction and collaboration has particular relevance to coaching. In the coaching model development process, coaches are encouraged to learn by doing and to discuss their interactions with their colleagues.

Humanism and Learning as a Process
Carl Rogers and Abraham Maslow

Humanist theorists, such as Carl Rogers and Abraham Maslow, recognized that conditions of the interpersonal environment can permit, encourage, and nurture learning. Maslow viewed the goal of learning to be self-actualization, "the full use of talents, capacities, potentialities, etc." (1987, 150). To encourage growth toward this goal, he emphasized the importance of safety. Maslow noted that individuals feel unthreatened, autonomous and ready to choose the unknown if the environment gratifies their needs for safety, a sense of belonging, and respect.

Rogers focused on the development of "fully functioning people," conceptualizing a learner-centered approach to education. Based on the belief that educational situations promote significant learning when threats to the self of the learner are minimized, Rogers emphasized the importance of making the climate psychologically safe for learners.

> The only man who is educated is the man who has learned how to learn; the man who has learned how to adapt and change; the man who has realized that no knowledge is secure, that only the process of *seeking* knowledge gives a basis for security. Changingness, a reliance on process rather than upon static knowledge, is the only thing that makes any sense as a goal for education in the modern world (Rogers 1989, 304).

Rogers believed that the aim of education is the facilitation of change and learning. To accomplish this, he placed special emphasis on learners moving toward valuing self-direction "being a process," and openness to inner and outer experience.

> If the human species is to survive at all on this globe, the human being must become more readily adaptive to new problems and situations, must be able to select that which is valuable for development and survival out of new and complex situations, must be accurate in his appreciation of reality if he is to make such selections (Rogers 1989, 183).

Rogers reflected on his own action choices: "Why does it appeal to me to try the unknown, to gamble on something new, when I could easily settle for ways of doing things that I know from past experience would work very satisfactorily?" (1989, 41). He acknowledged his own need to counter boredom with sameness and sureness, then added:

> But perhaps the major reason I am willing to take chances is that I have found that in doing so, whether I succeed or fail, I *learn*. Learning, especially learning from experience, has been a prime element in making my life worthwhile. Such learning helps me to expand (Rogers 1989, 42).

Concepts from adult learning theories, including the role of the learner's experience and self-directed learning, are germane to the process of coaching model development. In the next chapter, you will find guidelines for coaching model development derived from these learning theories.

TRANSFORMATIVE LEARNING

Exploring principles from transformative learning theories about critical reflection and informed action can stimulate reflection on your own assumptions, beliefs, and action choices in a coaching context. Highlights follow of the work of major learning theorists—select transformative learning theories that are particularly relevant to coaching. These include:

- Transformative learning and critical reflection—*Jack Mezirow*
- Education for social change and praxis—action and reflection—*Paulo Freire*

Transformative Learning and Critical Reflection
Jack Mezirow

Principles from *transformative learning* practice offer insights into the adult learner's process of making meaning, taking action, and changing. Transformative learning focuses on the adult learner's mental construction of experience and inner meaning. The development of transformative learning theory began in 1978 with Jack Mezirow's research study of women returning to community college after an extended hiatus. His findings suggested that adulthood is a transformative process in which adults distance themselves from childhood roles, reframe their perspectives and act on redefined perspectives, then become more engaged in life with a greater sense of self-direction. Mezirow conceptualized transformative learning as a process by which adult learners transform their:

> taken-for-granted frames of reference (meaning perspectives, habits of mind, mind-sets) to make them more inclusive, discriminating, open, emotionally capable of change, and reflective so that they may generate beliefs and opinions that will prove more true or justified to guide action (2000, 7–8).

Mezirow initiated the development of transformative learning as a learning theory with the publication of his 1978 research study. He describes the findings of his study:

> The major theoretical finding of the study was the identification of perspective transformation as the central learning process occurring in the personal development of women participating in these college programs. By becoming critically aware of the context—biographical, historical, cultural—of their beliefs and feelings about themselves and their role in society, the women

could effect a change in the way they had tacitly structured their assumptions and expectations. This change constituted a learning transformation; the process resulting from it was designated transformative learning (Mezirow 2000, xi–xii).

The transformative learning model advanced by Mezirow highlights the role of critical reflection, rational discourse, and the capacity of adult learners to take informed, responsible, creative action. Drawing on the work of German philosopher Jurgen Habermas, Mezirow described two major learning domains: communicative learning and instrumental learning. Communicative learning is concerned with what others mean when they communicate about their values, feelings, and intentions. It involves becoming critically reflective of the communicator's assumptions. Instrumental learning refers to the acquisition of technical knowledge. Learning often involves elements of both domains. Mezirow positioned reflection as a process for releasing dysfunctional beliefs, and discourse as a process for validating beliefs. Both processes are integral to coaching.

Education for Social Change and Praxis—Action and Reflection
Paulo Freire

Mezirow's theory of transformative learning was significantly influenced by the Brazilian educator, Paulo Freire. While Mezirow's attention was on personal transformation, Freire's was on social transformation. Central to Freire's theory of *education for social change* is the concept of praxis, a process of moving back and forth in a critical way between action and reflection (2000). This process increases learners' awareness of the socio-cultural forces that shape their lives. Similarly, Brookfield pointed out that central to adult learning is the process of engaging in a "continuous and alternating process of investigation and exploration, followed by action grounded in this exploration, followed by reflection on this action, followed by further investigation and exploration, followed by further action, and so on" (1986, 15).

Freire's social transformation theory and Mezirow's personal transformation theory share an emphasis on changes in consciousness through critical reflection, discourse, and reflective action. Freire's concept of *conscientization* is a process of increasing awareness of one's situation by moving from the lowest level of consciousness to the highest level of critical consciousness through dialogue and action. Similarly, Mezirow's concept of critical reflection involves analysis of problems, discourse, and reflective action. Common to both approaches is the adult learner becoming aware of assumptions, beliefs, and values and then transforming them into a new perspective or level of consciousness.

In addition to Freire and Mezirow, Brookfield wrote extensively about the form and process of *critical reflection* for adult learners. He placed special emphasis on relativism and students learning to evaluate and distinguish among multiple options. "This awareness that the supposed givens of work conduct, relationships, and political allegiances are, in fact, culturally constructed, means that adults will come to question many aspects of their professional, personal and political lives" (Brookfield 1986, 10–11). Brookfield's approach to adult education encouraged learners to understand and appreciate that knowledge is culturally transmitted and relative. "The point is that education is centrally concerned with the development of a critically aware frame of mind, not with the uncritical assimilation of previously defined skills or bodies of knowledge" (Brookfield 1986, 17).

Freire, Mezirow, and Brookfield agree on the importance of thinking critically about social conditions, constructing solutions through dialogue, and taking action. The key in praxis is the relationship between reflection and action, made possible through dialogue. Reflection and action play a central role in the coaching model development process and will be discussed in more detail throughout this book.

CROSS-CULTURAL LEARNING

When you examine the principles from cross-cultural learning theories, you increase your awareness of individual and cultural differences encountered in coaching situations. Highlights follow of the work of cross-cultural learning theorists—select theories that are relevant to the process of developing your own model and working with it to improve coaching effectiveness. These include:

- Cultural differences and value dimensions—*Geert Hofstede*
- Identity negotiation, values, and self-concept—*Stella Ting-Toomey*
- Intercultural management and cultural dilemmas—*Fons Trompenaars and Charles Hampden-Turner*
- Intercultural relations and cultural patterns—*Edward Stewart and Milton Bennett*
- Intercultural communication and cultural uniqueness—*Marshall Singer*
- Cultural identity development and cultural learning—*Peter Adler*

- Mindful learning and multiple perspectives—*Ellen Langer*

Cultural Differences and Value Dimensions
Geert Hofstede

Individuals express culture through their values. Their values in turn affect their attitudes about whatever behaviors they consider most appropriate and effective in each situation. The study of adult learning explores the cultural orientation of learners, as reflected in the complex interplay of their values, attitudes, and behavior.

To gain a better understanding of differences and similarities in *cultural values*, social scientist Geert Hofstede conducted a massive study in a U.S. multinational corporation (IBM) with subsidiaries in 50 countries and three regions (Arabic-speaking countries, East Africa, and West Africa). He surveyed 116,000 executives two times, and came up with four cultural value dimensions: affiliation–achievement, certainty–uncertainty, individualism–collectivism, low power distance–high power distance.

The certainty–uncertainty value dimension is particularly relevant to understanding the experience of entering new and unique situations. It measures the extent to which people of different cultures prefer unstructured, risky, ambiguous, or unpredictable situations; or prefer to live by rules, regulations, and controls. This value orientation was investigated in IBM and other organizations that are structure-oriented with a preference for strong codes of behaviors and management practices, and ones that are risk-oriented and encourage individuals to take initiative.

As an example, Hofstede explained the important distinction between uncertainty avoidance and risk avoidance:

> Uncertainty avoidance should not be confused with risk avoidance: uncertainty is to risk as anxiety is to fear. Fear and risk are both focused on something specific: an object in the case of fear, an event in the case of risk. Risk is often expressed as a percentage of probability that a particular event may happen. Anxiety and uncertainty are both diffuse feelings. Anxiety, as was argued earlier, has no object. Uncertainty has no probability attached to it. It is a situation in which anything can happen and we have no idea what. As soon as uncertainty is expressed as risk, it ceases to be a source of anxiety. It may become a source of fear, but it may also be accepted as routine, like the risks of driving a car or practicing a sport. . . . Even more than reducing risk, uncertainty avoidance leads to a reduction of ambiguity. Uncertainty avoiding

cultures shun ambiguous situations. People in such cultures look for a structure in their organizations, institutions and relationships which makes events clearly interpretable and predictable (Hofstede 1997, 116).

Hofstede's groundbreaking research described dimensions of difference and underscored the influence of cultural values on behavior. Throughout this book, coaches will find questions and activities to assist them in clarifying their individual cultural orientation, and the core values that drive their behavior in the coaching context.

Identity Negotiation, Values, and Self-Concept
Stella Ting-Toomey

The *identity negotiation* perspective highlights the connection between cultural values and self-concept. Stella Ting-Toomey integrated research studies that draw from the work of social identity theory (social psychology), symbolic interactionism (sociology), and identity negotiation and relational dialectics (communication theory and research). She identified eight identity domains that play an important role in intercultural interactions:

- four self-image domains: cultural, ethnic, gender, and personal identities
- four identity domains that change depending on the situation: role, relational, facework, and symbolic interactional identities.

Ting-Toomey emphasized the complex diversity of identities within every individual. "Identity is viewed as reflective self-images constructed, experienced, and communicated by the individuals within a culture and in a particular interaction situation" (Ting-Toomey 1999, 39).

A core assumption of the identity negotiation theory is: "Individuals in all cultures or ethnic groups have the basic motivation needs for identity security, trust, inclusion, connection, and stability on both group-based and person-based identity levels" (Ting-Toomey 1999, 40). She also examined Hofstede's uncertainty avoidance value dimension by relating it to an individual member of a culture who feels threatened by an uncertain or unknown situation and is trying to avoid it. From her identity negotiation perspective, Ting-Toomey found that the personality factors of high tolerance for ambiguity and personal flexibility promote identity security and inclusion. Fundamental to her identity negotiation theory is the belief that effective intercultural communicators need to learn the value systems that influence others' self-concepts. Ting-Toomey's work raises the issue of cultural sensitivity and the importance for coaches to become aware of their own individual cultural orientation.

Intercultural Management and Cultural Dilemmas
Fons Trompenaars and Charles Hampden-Turner

To reconcile opposite ends of the value dimensions, *intercultural management* experts Fons Trompenaars and Charles Hampden-Turner recommended using the criterion of synergy. The word *synergy*, which comes from the Greek word *sunergos*, means "to work with." Trompenaars and Hampden-Turner suggested that "when two values work with one another they are mutually facilitating and enhancing" (1998, 216).

They organized their research on cultural differences into seven key dimensions: orientations to time; feelings; nature; context and communication; relationships and rules; the group and the individual; achievement and ascription. By *achievement* they meant accomplishments or track record. By *ascription* they meant status attributed by birth, kinship, gender, age, connections, or education. They described ways in which managers can cope with differing cultural values in various business contexts. One of their examples was the "achieved-ascribed status" dimension. In this dimension, people work in a "virtuous circle": when people ascribe importance to a project, it is more likely that the working group will be inspired to achieve that project. Then, the achievement of that project makes it more likely that senior management will ascribe great importance to the same or related projects. The ascribing of importance to the project again leads to high levels of achievement, and the process continues.

Trompenaars and Hampden-Turner believed that all societies ascribe status and strive to achieve; however, where the cycle begins varies:

> Those who "start" with ascribing usually ascribe not just status but set high expectations for future success or achievement and thereby bring it about. Those who "start" with achievement usually start to ascribe importance and priority to the people and projects which have been successful (Trompenaars and Hampden-Turner 1998, 118).

They believed that opposing values can be complementary and reconcilable. "Once we are aware of our own mental models and cultural predispositions and can respect and understand that those of another culture are legitimately different, then it becomes possible to reconcile differences" (Trompenaars and Hampden-Turner 1998, 205). Their approach to resolving dilemmas focuses on integrating rather than polarizing cultural value differences. In their view, searching into and resolving dilemmas is a form of learning that requires creativity and innovation. When applied to coaching, the theories of Trompenaars and Hampden-Turner highlight the importance of examining, respecting, and appreciating cultural value differences.

Intercultural Relations and Cultural Patterns
Edward Stewart and Milton Bennett

When Americans are educated to recognize that they come from a culture, they strengthen their ability to relate to and learn from others who are culturally different. This suggestion was made by Edward C. Stewart and Milton J. Bennett in their detailed analysis of American cultural patterns and implications for effective *intercultural relations* (1991).

Stewart and Bennett wrote about the emerging awareness of interdependence with others. They referenced Robert Bellah's work in which he terms the American social norm of self-reliance as "mythic individualism" (Bellah et al. 1985, 144–7). Stewart, Bennett, and Bellah believed that what began in America as utilitarian self-reliance became, in some cases, an avoidance of dependence. Bellah wrote:

> We find ourselves not independently of other people and institutions but through them. We never get to the bottom of our selves on our own. We discover who we are face-to-face and side-by-side with others in work, love, and learning [. . .] We are parts of a larger whole that we can neither forget nor imagine in our own image without paying a high price. If we are not to have a self that hangs in the void, slowly twisting in the wind, these are issues we cannot ignore (1985, 84).

Cultivating cultural understanding is critical for coaches who are developing their own coaching model, but it can be challenging because cultural patterns are often deeply rooted and sometimes beyond one's conscious awareness. Many of the reflective activities in this book are designed specifically to facilitate the coach's process of increasing cultural self-awareness.

Intercultural Communication and Cultural Uniqueness
Marshall Singer

Essential to a discussion of coaching are issues related to connection with others and one's individuality, as well as how an individual's unique set of experiences and perspectives affect interpersonal communication. Marshall Singer, who researched perception and identity, pointed out that every identity group has a culture of its own, and every individual is a part of many different identity groups and cultures simultaneously. He stated that:

> because no person is a part of all and only the same groups as anyone else and because each person ranks the attitudes, values, and beliefs of the groups to which he or she belongs differently, which is what culture is all about, *each individual must be considered to be culturally unique* (Singer 1998, xiii).

Singer was aware that culture is a group-related phenomenon. Nevertheless, he believed that every interpersonal communication must to some extent be an intercultural communication because no two individuals share the exact same group memberships or ranking of importance to themselves of the group memberships they share.

The concept of cultural uniqueness is emphasized throughout this book. Coaches must be sensitive not only to the cultural uniqueness of the people they coach, but also to their own cultural uniqueness.

Cultural Identity Development and Cultural Learning
Peter Adler

Peter S. Adler recognized the profound complexity of *cultural identity development*. He reflected on the need to remain flexible, open, and committed to a world view that extends beyond one's own culture, inclusive of a multiplicity of realities. Adler described a multicultural person who is always in flux, continually redefining one's self, responding, adapting, and changing in the face of new experience and contact with the world. This person engages in cultural learning and cultural unlearning, a series of experiments and explorations to realign needs and expectations to fit the context. Through this process, the multicultural personality transcends the permanent, fixed, traditional structure of cultural identity, and undergoes shifts in outlook, values, and actions:

> The rise of the multicultural person is a significant phenomenon and represents a new psychocultural style of self-process. . . . Values and attitudes, worldview and beliefs are always in reformation, dependent more on the necessities of experience than on the predispositions of a given culture. . . . He or she is always in a state of "becoming" or "un-becoming" something different from before while yet mindful of the grounding in his or her primary

cultural reality. . . . Multicultural persons, like great philosophers in any age, can never accept totally the demands of any one culture, nor are they free from the conditioning of their culture. Their psychocultural style must always be relational and in movement, enabling them to look at their own original culture from an outsider's perspective. This tension gives rise to a dynamic, passionate, and critical posture in the face of totalistic ideologies, systems, and movements (Adler 1998, 235–6).

Adler's research takes on particular significance for coaches who continually engage with people whose cultural orientations are different from their own. By critically reflecting on their own cultural views and alternatives to them, coaches can move toward a world view that includes recognition of the full range of human experience.

Mindful Learning and Multiple Perspectives
Ellen Langer

Ellen Langer recognized the instability of experience that can differ in each moment and within each person. She responded to social science's approach to identifying stable phenomena by identifying the difference between intelligence and *mindfulness*. Whereas intelligence is "developed from an observing expert's perspective, which focuses on stable categories," mindfulness is "developed from an actor's ability to experience personal control by shifting perspectives." Langer stated:

> When we are mindful, we implicitly or explicitly (1) view a situation from several perspectives, (2) see information presented in the situation as novel, (3) attend to the context in which we are perceiving the information, and eventually (4) create new categories through which this information may be understood (1997, 111).

Langer wrote about uncertainty and creative thought. From a mindful perspective, uncertainty is seen as creating the conditions that make it possible to discover meaning. She advocated a *sideways learning* approach designed to maintain a mindful state. This involves openness to novelty, alertness to distinction, sensitivity to different contexts, awareness of multiple perspectives, and an orientation in the present.

Inspired by Ellen Langer's concept of *mindful learning*, Stella Ting-Toomey's identity negotiation theory included the component of *mindful intercultural communication*. A core assumption of Ting-Toomey's theory underscores two key concepts: "the first is that mindful intercultural communication has three components—knowledge, motivation, and skills; the second is that mindful intercultural communication refers to the appropriate, effective, and satisfactory management of desired shared meanings and goals in an intercultural episode" (1999, 48). The practice of mindful intercultural communication requires paying attention to one's own beliefs, values, assumptions, and behaviors, and simultaneously, being aware of the other person's cultural frame of reference. As mentioned in an earlier section, Ting-Toomey stressed the importance of staying open to unfamiliar behavior and situations, and using mental flexibility to rethink assumptions about one's self and the world.

Both Langer and Ting-Toomey emphasized that mindful communicators need to learn to view and understand situations from multiple perspectives. For coaches who are developing and applying their coaching models, this openness to different points of view is essential.

SUMMARY

Many theories and viewpoints inform this book's approach to coaching model development and application. This chapter has presented some conceptual frameworks from the fields of education, culture, communication, and international management. Beginning with the relevance of learning to the coaching process and theories of adult learning, it focused on the fundamental assumptions about making meaning that are unique to adulthood. It then explored transformative learning theory, which considers how adults learn to assess their assumptions and change their frames of reference to guide future action. Themes from research studies on transformative learning included perspective transformation and the role of critical reflection. It ended with a review of theories and research studies that look at cultural differences and how certain groups and individuals respond to and make meaning of significant experiences. All are concerned with direct experience, awareness, and individual learner differences.

"To invent one's own meaning means knowing how to find it" (Barba 1995, 48). Central to the development of a coaching model is the process of learning how to learn, and learning to negotiate and act on one's own values, feelings, and meanings. The intellectual origins presented in this chapter set the context for this process.

You, the coach, are an active learner. As you develop and refine your own coaching model, consider how you can draw on the learning theories that resonate with you. The next step towards your model is to understand theory-based guidelines for the process of model development. In the next chapter, you will find questions to guide self-reflection. You can also use them as the basis for discussions with a colleague. As a result of exploring your responses to these questions, you will make explicit the perspectives and strengths you bring, consciously or not, to the people you coach.

3

THEORY-BASED GUIDELINES

How do theories of adult, transformative, and cross-cultural learning apply to coaching models? Based on an analysis of the theories previously presented, this chapter proposes ways those theories can guide the development of your own coaching model. Sections in this chapter include:

- Experience: Use your personal and professional experiences as a resource.
- Reflection: Act and reflect to continue the learning process.
- Reflective capabilities and practices.

By using theory-based guidelines, you can develop a model that incorporates your unique perspectives, strengths, and the individual and cultural influences on your approach to coaching.

EXPERIENCE: USE YOUR PERSONAL AND PROFESSIONAL EXPERIENCES AS A RESOURCE

The theories of Knowles, Argyris and Schon, Brookfield, and Kolb, summarized in the previous chapter, focused on the central role of experience in the learning process. The breadth and depth of your life experiences are crucial content that you can draw on as you develop your coaching model. By capitalizing on your past and current experience, you can learn a great deal about what you bring to the coaching context and how you approach coaching interactions.

Educational theories emphasize that adults have accumulated a large reservoir of experience. Adults learn new knowledge, skills, and attitudes best in relation to that experience. As noted by Brookfield, "exploration of new ideas, skills or bodies of knowledge do not take place in a vacuum but are set within the context of learners' past, current and future experiences" (1986, 15). You can frame your model in terms that are accessible to you, based on your past and current base of experience. The guidelines related to experience hold that the richest resource for coaching model development can be found within you.

In this approach to coaching model development, you are encouraged to analyze your unique set of personal and professional experiences. You can begin by engaging in a process of self-inquiry or by discussing with a friend or a colleague four aspects of your experience:

1. your *participation* in meaningful experiences;
2. your *social connections*, the bonds you form and the interactions you have with others;
3. your *interests and expertise*; and
4. the *contexts* or settings in which your experiences take place.

Additionally, you can identify and heighten your awareness of four individual and cultural factors that influence your perspectives and the meanings you make of your experiences:

1. your *cultural background*;
2. *communication behavior norms*—the most common, accepted patterns of behavior;
3. your *core values and beliefs*; and
4. your *individual traits*.

A discussion of the four aspects of experience follows. You will find questions for reflection after each section. Some questions focus on data, external reality, and others focus on your internal relationship to

Figure 3.1 Four Aspects of Experience

the data. By exploring your unique set of experiences, you can clarify your thoughts about your own approach to coaching. This facilitates the coaching model development process.

Analyze Your Participation

You have participated in many different kinds of personal and professional experiences throughout your lifetime. The concept of participation, as used here, refers to an active process of meaningful engagement with the world. By analyzing your participation in significant experiences, you can gain insights into when you are most open, engaged, and focused. John Dewey, a pragmatist and educational philosopher, writes about openness to inner and outer experience, "In a certain sense every experience should do something to prepare a person for later experiences of a deeper and more expansive quality" (1938, 47).

An effective way to begin developing your coaching model is to examine your participation in experiences that are meaningful to you. Consider the role that participation played in the development of Gallwey's coaching model, as an example (discussed in Chapter 2). Gallwey engaged in meaningful teaching and learning interactions with his tennis students, explored ways to enhance their performance, and experimented with words and actions during these sessions. As a result, he developed his Inner Game coaching model and applied it to a wide range of audiences.

Questions for reflection: Participation

- What personal or professional experiences have you participated in that were most engaging?
- How did you participate in these experiences? What made them particularly engaging and meaningful?

Analyze Your Social Connections

Your participation in personal and professional experiences allows you to make social connections. The social bonds you form and the interactions you have with others influence your choices. You are affected by the connections you make. When you connect with others, their actions, thoughts, and feelings have an impact on you; and, in turn, yours have an impact on them. Learning occurs in a social context. Mezirow notes that "dialogue or communicative action allows us to relate to the world around us, to other people, and to our own intentions, feelings, and desires" (1991, 65). Making sense of experience is made possible through connecting with others and engaging in meaningful dialogue. Together, you engage in a kind of shared inquiry.

It is vital to become aware of the learning dialogues you have with key people in your life and how they influence your ways of thinking and acting. Integral to the coaching model development process is an analysis of your significant social connections and the ways they have shaped you. How you engage in learning with the people in your life will influence how you approach the mutual learning that takes place during coaching interactions. Consider the example of the NYU graduate student in a joint degree program in law and business who developed a model for coaching high achievers. By participating in professional and academic experiences and connecting with her high-achieving peers, she developed her own coaching model for a specific target audience.

Questions for reflection: Social connections

- What significant individual or group connections have you made as a result of your experiences?
- What have you learned from these individuals or groups that influences the way you approach coaching?

Analyze Your Interests and Expertise

An analysis of your experiences involves identifying your areas of interest and expertise. When you are engaged in experiences that matter to you, you pay great attention to detail and remain focused on the needs of the moment. Your intention to achieve a particular goal and your commitment to adapt to changes, as needed, drive your actions. The word *intention*, derived from the Latin *intentio* meaning "to stretch out," suggests a combination of purpose and a determination to pursue it. From Latin *committere*, meaning to connect, *commitment* suggests a willing pursuit to carry out a course of action.

Directing your attention to areas of interest and expertise will provide you with a rich storehouse of material for your coaching model. Consider Peltier's executive coaching practice. A licensed psychologist, a professor of psychology, and an executive coach, Peltier draws on his clinical experience and expertise in psychoanalysis to guide his work with corporate executives. He applies his expertise to his coaching practice in the business environment.

Questions for reflection: Interests and expertise
• What do you consider to be your major areas of expertise and interest? • What are some ways to bring your strengths in those areas to a coaching situation?

Analyze the Contexts

Many factors give meaning to your experiences. Context is an important variable. Typically, people think of context only as a physical setting—a classroom, a private office, or a corporate conference room. It is also important to think about the relational and situational contexts in which communication occurs, including the social roles and positions of the people interacting. Communication occurs in contexts created by the physical, cultural, historical, relational, or situational aspects of a situation.

Coaches, as communicators, work in multilayered contexts, i.e. settings, in which their communication takes place. Multilayered contexts frame our interactions, set up expectations for communication, and significantly affect our communication behavior.

Anthropologist Edward T. Hall explains what people pay attention to (and what they don't pay attention to) by classifying communication as "high context" and "low context." He defines context as "the information that surrounds an event; it is inextricably bound up with the meaning of the event" (Hall and Hall 1990, 6). In high context communication, meaning is conveyed through multiple contexts (e.g. historical, relational, and situational contexts) and non-verbal signals. The information in high context communication is mostly in the setting, not in the words. Meaning can be found in the use of space, title, age, affiliations, education, and non-verbal signals, such as silence and gestures. In contrast, the meaning in low context communication is conveyed through explicit verbal messages. The information in low context communication is mostly transmitted in words. Hall explains:

> A high context (HC) communication or message is one in which most of the information is already in the person, while very little is in the coded, explicit, transmitted part of the message. A low context (LC) communication is just the opposite; i.e. the mass of the information is vested in the explicit code. Twins who have grown up together can and do communicate more economically

(HC) than two lawyers in a courtroom during a trial (LC), a mathematician programming a computer, two politicians drafting legislation, two administrators writing a regulation (1976, 91).

When developing and applying your own coaching model, it is important to pay attention to contextual factors that may influence your coaching interactions. These may include the industry, organization, organizational dynamics and structure, subunit culture, recent events, and current climate. Some coaches build awareness of context and ability to respond to different contexts into their model. Consider the importance of context in Kemp's adventure-based coaching model discussed in Chapter 2. Each challenge takes place in a different context. In his adventure-based coaching process, cognitive and behavioral learning from the adventure experience in one particular context is then transferred to similar situations and contexts in the client's real world.

Questions for reflection: Contexts

- How can your awareness of high context messages strengthen your effectiveness as a communicator?
- What contextual factors influence your coaching interactions?

A discussion of the four individual and cultural factors that influence your perspectives and the meanings you make of your experiences follows. These factors are:

1. your *cultural background*;
2. *communication behavior norms*—the most common, accepted patterns of behavior;
3. your *core values and beliefs*; and
4. your *individual traits*.

To identify and heighten your awareness of these factors, you will find questions for reflection after each section. By exploring your unique set of perspectives, you can clarify your thoughts about your own approach to coaching.

Analyze Your Cultural Background

The importance of developing awareness of the powerful cultural forces that influence your actions cannot be underestimated. This awareness involves recognizing and appreciating your cultural background and

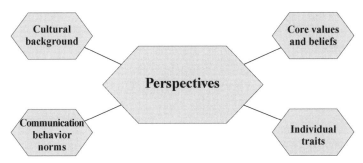

Figure 3.2 Four Individual and Cultural Factors

identity. An analysis of the numerous cultural groups that you belong to is a step in that direction. Cultural groups are defined here as people who, through intragroup communication, have arrived at shared understandings of how to perceive their social environment and how to solve the key problems of life. Such understandings have been transmitted from one generation to the next as recommended ways of thinking and acting. They inform your beliefs, values, attitudes, and behaviors. You may consider yourself to be a member of a particular industry, a discipline, a profession, an organization, a geographic region, a nation, ethnic or religious group, a neighborhood, a family, as well as other groups.

Too often people think about cultural differences and cultural identity primarily in terms of nationality, but your sense of self may come from many other group memberships that are more relevant and important to you. Daphne A. Jameson, a faculty member at Cornell University, suggests a typology of identity groups that includes six categories:

1. vocation—occupation, profession, organization;
2. class—economic, social, educational;
3. geography—nationality, region, density identification, residence;
4. philosophy—religious, political, other philosophies;
5. language—first, dialect, other languages; and
6. biological traits with cultural aspects—race, ethnicity, gender, sexual orientation, health, age (2007, 211).

In the approach to coaching model development presented in this book, it is essential to acknowledge the cultural forces that influence your orientation to coaching. Identifying the groups to which you belong is an important step in understanding how your cultural identity and background informs your ways of thinking and behaving.

Consider the part-time MBA student in Chapter 2 who identified himself as a project manager in a financial services company, responsible for implementing technology systems. With a clear understanding of his own and his organization's norms of thinking and behaving, he created a coaching model to empower his team to make decisions and solve problems on their own.

Questions for reflection: Cultural background

- How would you describe your cultural background? With which cultural groups are you most identified?
- How might your cultural background influence the ways you think and act in a coaching situation?

Analyze Communication Behavior Norms

Culture is shared by members of a group. Hofstede sees culture as "the collective programming of the mind which distinguishes the members of one human group from another . . . the interactive aggregate of common characteristics that influence a human group's response to its environment" (1980, 25). It is most important to understand that culture influences your behavior and, in turn, your behavior influences culture. This cycle of influence is continuous. Although culture is ubiquitous, multidimensional, and complex, you can define your group memberships and you can analyze the cultural forces (external structures, beliefs and values, and underlying assumptions) that operate within these groups. Edgar Schein believes that leaders in organizations must understand the complexities of the cultures in which they are embedded if they are to lead, managing culture rather than letting culture manage them. According to Schein, "Overt behavior is always determined both by the cultural predisposition (the perceptions, thoughts, and feelings that are patterned) and by the situational contingencies that arise from the immediate external environment" (2004, 19).

During the process of developing a coaching model, it is important to explore your cultural orientation, as reflected in the complex interplay of your values, beliefs, and behavior. This includes examining the forms of communication behavior considered most appropriate and effective in any given circumstance. For example, managers may communicate respect for their employees in different ways, depending on their cultural orientation. Some may communicate respect by focusing only on the employee's behavior at work, whereas others will focus on their employee's behavior in both their private and professional lives. Another example is non-verbal communication behavior. The gestures, looks, and physical actions that a manager from one culture uses may not be the same as that of a manager from another culture. As you saw in Chapter 2, Whitmore derived and developed the GROW model from his experience using a series of non-judgmental reflective questions, first with people in sports performance situations and then with business people in problem-solving situations. Using the GROW sequence with effective coaching questions builds awareness, responsibility, self-belief, and self-motivation in the people being coached.

Questions for reflection: Communication behavior norms

- What are the communication behavior norms in your organization or professional discipline?
- What main ways of communicating characterize your approach to coaching?

Analyze Your Core Values and Beliefs

You express culture through your values; your values, in turn, affect the behaviors you consider most appropriate and effective in each situation. Your core values are principles that are intrinsically or extrinsically desirable. They not only reflect your beliefs about what is right and wrong but they also influence your behavior. Social psychologist Milton Rokeach defined a value as "a learned organization of rules for making choices and for resolving conflicts" (1973, 161).

Florence Kluckhohn and Fred Strodtbeck, who researched cultural patterns, concluded that people look to their cultures to answer five basic questions:

1. What is the character of human nature?
2. What is the relation of humankind to nature?
3. What is the orientation to time?
4. What is the value placed on activity?
5. What is the relationship of people to each other?

Kluckhohn and Strodtbeck argue that people have universally shared concerns and cultures choose to address these concerns depending on their values. They identified five value orientations that can best be represented as points on a continuum: relational orientation (individual–group), time orientation (past–present–future), activity orientation (doing–being), man–nature orientation (dominant–harmony), and human nature orientation (good–evil). Kluckhohn and Strodtbeck theorized that every culture has a set of dominant or preferred value orientations (1961).

Expanding your awareness of your own core values and dominant beliefs (your convictions about what is right or true) is a vital practice for coaching model development and application. Your core values and beliefs have a significant impact on your communication behavior and will inform the way you choose to approach your coaching practice. Hunt and Weintraub's developmental coaching model for managers clearly reflects their core values of learning and development. Their model is structured around their belief that coaching is not the primary goal of most managers and, therefore, managers need a simple model that can be incorporated into their daily routine (Hunt and Weintraub 2002).

Questions for reflection: Core values and beliefs

- What are the core values that guide your actions in a coaching situation?
- What are your core beliefs about coaching?

Analyze Your Individual Traits

Your choices are shaped by many factors, including your individual history, social group membership, affiliations, genetic makeup, current circumstances, personal qualities, among others. Every coach is unique. Identifying your individual traits is as important as identifying the powerful cultural forces that influence the ways in which you experience the world and construct the meaning of your experiences. Through your participation in experiences and connection with others, you develop an awareness of your personal style, qualities, and competencies. As you engage in action with others in a variety of ways, you encounter your effect on them and on your social environment. You gain key insights about your strengths and how you can build on them. You also clarify your areas for improvement and particular qualities likely to be challenged and tested by particular situations. By engaging in the outer world and exploring new understandings in your experiences, you can expand your self-awareness.

An analysis of your individual traits is a vital practice for developing your coaching model. It is particularly useful to recognize that your strengths in excess can become your liabilities. Consider the four behavioral styles described by Thomas Crane, including a preference for one of the following:

1. "Collaborative style" of interacting: This person may have strengths that include being a team player, sensitive, flexible, and patient. In excess, these strengths may show up as a tendency to be non-confrontational, overly emotional, overly compliant, and unable to say no.
2. "Clarifying style": This person may have strengths that include being systematic, objective, thorough, and accurate. In excess, such a person might be data-bound, risk averse, tedious, and a perfectionist.
3. "Conducting style": This person may have strengths that include being an initiator, independent, disciplined, and organized. In excess, these strengths may lead to insensitivity, an autocratic style, impatience, and poor listening.
4. "Creative style": Someone who prefers this style may be enthusiastic, spontaneous, creative, and dynamic. In excess, the person can be seen as having poor follow-through, missing details, impulsive, and a poor planner (Crane and Patrick 2001, 149).

Self-awareness is a core competency for coach practitioners. Appreciation and respect for your individual traits is a mind-set that will predispose you to investigate your own behavior. You can increase your awareness of personal traits by doing reflective practices that bring your behavior into sharper focus. Consider Renwick's approach to coaching global executives by taking on different roles (described in Chapter 1). Renwick capitalizes on his own strengths, in particular his cognitive and behavioral flexibility. Based on the needs and cultural orientation of his clients, Renwick shifts between different roles that enhance his intercultural communication and coaching effectiveness.

Questions for reflection: Individual traits

- What individual traits do you consider to be your assets?
- What strengths in excess could become your liabilities?

REFLECTION: ACT AND REFLECT TO CONTINUE THE LEARNING PROCESS

Many of the learning theories summarized in Chapter 2 emphasize the importance of reflection, as well as experience. Reflection enables you to discover the meaning of your experience. An analysis of the theories involving some form of reflection reveals that learning is most effective when you take action and reflect on that action. The primary practice for coaching model development derived from learning theory is to engage in reflection. By acting and reflecting, you can make sense of your coaching experiences and understand the thinking that underlies your actions.

As discussed earlier, Freire uses the term *praxis*, a Greek word meaning "reflection with action." Each theorist discussed in Chapter 2 interprets the role and nature of reflection slightly differently. Particularly relevant to coaching model development are Kolb's reflective observation, Argyris' ladder of inference, Schon's reflection-in-action, Mezirow's critical reflection, and Langer's mindfulness.

Reflective Observation
Kolb's View on Reflection in the Experiential Learning Cycle

Central to Kolb's experiential learning cycle is reflective observation. After being involved in concrete experience, you reflect on and observe your experience from multiple perspectives. This part of the learning process suggests the vital importance of carefully observing data before making judgments and viewing issues from different perspectives to uncover meaning. In Kolb's view (1984), learning by reflecting is followed by abstract conceptualization; that is, logically analyzing ideas, planning systematically, and acting on an intellectual understanding of a situation. The next stage in the learning cycle is active experimentation; that is, learning by doing—getting things done, taking risks, and influencing people and events through action. According to Kolb, a meaningful learning experience involves all stages of the cycle. Some people may have a preference for one or more of the stages in this experiential learning cycle. For coaches, particularly those developing their coaching models, the practice of reflective observation is central. Kolb's experiential learning cycle is graphically depicted in Figure 3.3.

Ladder of Inference
Argyris' Tool for Reflection on the Reasoning Process

Argyris developed the ladder of inference (see Figure 3.4) as a tool to help people reflect on their reasoning process. The climb up the ladder

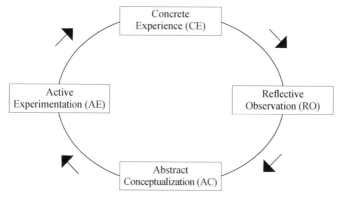

Figure 3.3 Kolb's Experiential Learning Model

begins with observing. Argyris notes that people select some data from the observed behavior. Next, they add some meaning to that data, make some assumptions based on those meanings, and draw some conclusions that they don't test and assume are true. From these assumptions, each person adopts new beliefs, sometimes misguided, and takes actions based on those beliefs. This mental reasoning process happens extremely quickly (Argyris 1990).

It is most important to understand that you can see the data at the bottom rung and the action taken at the top rung. The quick advance up the middle rungs happens only inside your head, without questioning or testing your reasoning. Your assumptions and conclusions lead to beliefs that inform what you select from observable data and the loop continues. Your beliefs reinforce the data you choose to observe. But it is not possible to stop making meaning based on your

Figure 3.4 Ladder of Inference
From THE FIFTH DISCIPLINE by Peter M. Senge, © 1990, 2006 by Peter M. Senge. Used by permission of Doubleday, a division of Random House, Inc.

past personal experiences and cultural influences. Throughout, you reflect on your thinking and reasoning process and generate new mental constructs. This ladder of inference can help you understand the thinking process of the people you coach. It can also guide your awareness of the inferences you make about what you observe and remind you to keep inference and observation separate.

Reflection-in-Action
Schon's View of a Process for Dealing with Unique, Uncertain Situations
As discussed in Chapter 2, Schon differentiates reflection *on* action, thinking back on an action taken, from reflection *in* action. Reflection-in-action involves a critical assessment of actions as they are taken. "In an *action-present*—a period of time, variable with the context, during which we can still make a difference to the situation at hand, our thinking serves to reshape what we are doing while we are doing it" (Schon 1983, 26).

For decades, Schon studied professional education and skillful practice based on reflection-in-action. He wrote about his study of education for reflective practice in four contexts—an architectural education program in a design studio, master classes in musical performance, psychoanalytic supervision, and a counseling and consulting skills program. He focused on the professional practice of "reflective practitioners" who deal with unique or uncertain situations by using existing knowledge to frame new ways of understanding. As he explains:

> They may ask themselves, for example, "What features do I notice when I recognize this thing? What are the criteria by which I make this judgment? What procedures am I enacting when I perform this skill? How am I framing the problem that I am trying to solve?" Usually reflection on knowing-in-action goes together with reflection on the stuff at hand . . . (Schon 1983, 50).

Schon's work highlights the importance of this reflective practice. As you develop and apply your own coaching model, you can incorporate this type of reflection. It will strengthen your ability to make new sense of unique situations by bringing your past experience and existing repertoire of knowledge and skills to bear on them.

Critical Reflection
Mezirow's View of Reflection in Transformative Learning Theory
Central to Mezirow's transformative learning theory is the role of critical reflection, including the capacity to be critically self-reflective and to use reflective judgment. According to Mezirow, "These adult

capabilities are indispensable for fully understanding the meaning of our experience and effective rational adult reasoning in critical discourse and communication learning" (2003, 60). He summarizes five functions of reflection:

1. Validating prior learning or attending to the grounds or justification for our beliefs
2. Solving or posing problems and transforming meaning schemes and perspectives
3. Reflecting on the *content* or description of a problem and the *process* or method of problem-solving—the purpose is to assess consciously what you know about taking the next step in a series of actions and to consider whether you will be "on course" in doing so
4. Reflecting on the *premise(s)* on which the problem is predicated—you can then move through cognitive structures by identifying and assessing presuppositions
5. Confirming, adding or transforming ways of interpreting experience (Mezirow 1991).

Understanding the nature and functions of reflection can heighten your awareness of how you, as well as the people you coach, solve problems and interpret experience.

Mindfulness
Langer's Interpretation of Reflection

Langer's mindfulness concept is similar to reflective action in that it involves paying attention to the content of a situation and multiple perspectives. Her extensive research studies characterize mindfulness as being open to new information, making new distinctions, being aware of more than one perspective, and focusing on process before outcome as well as the important role of context. In contrast, mind*less*ness is described as occurring when we rely only on past forms of action and previously conceived distinctions.

Langer writes about habitual action. She notes that mindless "experts" who perform a task repeatedly, without paying attention, become mentally lazy and that this can occur in almost any endeavor or profession. "We come to assume that we *can* do the task although we no longer know *how* we do it. In fact, questioning the process can have surprising results" (Langer 1989, 20). As you develop and apply your coaching model, you can draw on Langer's concept of mindfulness to guide your reflective thinking and increase the accuracy of your perception when encountering new and unique situations.

REFLECTIVE CAPABILITIES AND PRACTICES

Two types of reflective capabilities and practices are useful to coaches and managers who are developing and applying their coaching model. These are: *after-action reflection* and *real-time reflection*. The first type, after-action reflection, involves reflecting on:

1. **What** you think, do, feel, and say in a given circumstance
2. **How** you think, act, feel, and communicate in a given circumstance
3. **Why** you think, act, feel, and communicate as you do and the reasons for your choices in a given circumstance

In short, after-action reflection helps you understand the meaning of your experience by examining what has happened and how you understand it.

The second type, real-time reflection, involves reflecting and experimenting while in situations. Experimenting with new strategies of action and testing new forms of understanding while in situations can lead to an enhancement of your performance capabilities. During an interaction, you can draw information from the situation while in the situations by listening, observing, and suspending action and control until the moment of response.

Formulating new responses to dynamic interactions demands both cognitive and behavioral flexibility. In addition, it requires your attentiveness to continually changing conditions. You can confront uncertainties and actively respond with real-time reflection and experimentation. By observing and responding with honest inquiry, you can gather information and try out new actions to test your understanding of the situations. Honest inquiry, as used here, refers to seeing, hearing, staying in the moments of uncertainty, and not jumping to conclusions.

When you apply your model in coaching situations with clients or employees, real-time reflection is particularly useful. Real-time reflection requires you to experiment with words and actions while in the situation. It is a way for you to respond to open-ended situations through observing, listening, and attending to the details of the moment before testing new strategies of action and ways of framing problems. The capacity to rest momentarily in ambiguity and temporarily suspend action before making choices and taking action is vitally important for coaches.

Reflection is central to the process of coaching model development and application. You need to engage in reflection in order to explore

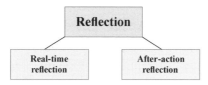

Figure 3.5 Reflective Capabilities and Practices

complexities, experiment with words and actions while in situations, learn from your actions, and come to a greater understanding of yourself and others. When you develop and apply your coaching model, reflect during and after actions. Reflection continues the learning process and facilitates the discovery of meanings.

SUMMARY

This chapter has described guidelines for coaching model development derived from theories of adult, transformative, and cross-cultural learning.

First, theory-based guidelines for capitalizing on past and current experience were presented. Students of coaching, coach practitioners, and managers can begin the process of developing a coaching model with an analysis of four aspects of their own experience (participation, social connections, interests and expertise, and contexts); and four individual and cultural factors that influence their perspectives and the perceived meaning of their experiences (cultural background, communication behavior norms, core values and beliefs, and individual traits).

Table 3.1 contains a summary of questions for reflection that were included in this chapter. Discussing these questions with a colleague can lead to productive conversations and new insights about your own approach to coaching.

Next, reflective practices derived from learning theories, including Kolb's reflective observation, Argyris' ladder of inference, Schon's reflection-in-action, Mezirow's critical reflection, and Langer's mindfulness, were described. The final section of this chapter has identified two primary reflective capabilities and practices for coaching model development: reflection after action and real-time reflection.

Part I of this book has introduced an approach to coaching model development. You have reviewed ideas that are fundamental to understanding coaching models, theories that lay the foundation for model development, and theory-based guidelines for the process of developing your own personalized model. Part II provides information and

Table 3.1
Coaching Model Development: Questions for Reflection and Discussion

Participation Analysis
- What personal or professional experiences have you participated in that were most engaging?
- How did you participate in these experiences? What made them particularly engaging and meaningful?

Social Connections Analysis
- What significant individual or group connections have you made as a result of your experiences?
- What have you learned from these individuals or groups that influences the way you approach coaching?

Interests and Expertise Analysis
- What do you consider to be your major areas of expertise and interest?
- What are some ways to bring your strengths in those areas to a coaching situation?

Context Analysis
- How can your awareness of high context messages strengthen your effectiveness as a communicator?
- What contextual factors influence your coaching interactions?

Cultural Background Analysis
- How would you describe your cultural background? With which cultural groups are you most identified?
- How might your cultural background influence the ways you think and act in a coaching situation?

Communication Behavior Analysis
- What are the communication behavior norms in your organization or professional discipline?
- What main ways of communicating characterize your approach to coaching?

Values and Beliefs Analysis
- What are the core values that guide your actions in a coaching situation?
- What are your core beliefs about coaching?

Individual Traits Analysis
- What individual traits do you consider to be your assets?
- What strengths in excess could become your liabilities?

practical strategies for you to develop your own personalized coaching model. The next chapter focuses on four main functions of a coaching model and will introduce you to some personalized coaching models developed by practitioners and corporate managers.

Part II
The Coaching Model

4

COACHING MODEL FUNCTIONS
AND CHARACTERISTICS

This chapter explores the functions of a coaching model. The model promotes understanding of a coaching approach. It assists the practitioner or manager in navigating a coaching process and planning for improved effectiveness as a coach. In this chapter, you will see some examples of models developed by practitioners and managers, based on their values, interests, and preferred approaches to coaching. As you will see, the models are different, but all share essential characteristics.

FOUR FUNCTIONS OF COACHING MODELS

Your coaching model is an intellectual device. Whether it is visual or verbal, it organizes your concepts about coaching and highlights only the key elements of the structure and process of coaching that you consider most important. Your model can guide your coaching decisions and actions, as well as facilitate the process of inquiry that is crucial to your ongoing learning and development as a coach.

Functionally, a coaching model:

1. Organizes a framework of ideas about coaching.
2. Highlights key elements of a coaching process.
3. Guides coaching decisions and actions.
4. Serves as a tool for continual learning by the coach.

Each of these four central functions is associated with an objective (see Table 4.1):

1. The organized framework promotes understanding of a coaching approach.
2. The highlighted elements facilitate the asking of questions.
3. The guide assists the practitioner or manager in navigating a coaching process.
4. The tool for learning facilitates insights and planning for improved coaching effectiveness.

Table 4.1
Four Central Functions of a Coaching Model

Function 1	Function 2	Function 3	Function 4
Organizes a framework of ideas about coaching	Highlights key elements of a coaching process	Guides coaching decisions and actions	Serves as a tool for continual learning
Objective	**Objective**	**Objective**	**Objective**
To promote understanding of a coaching approach by providing order and coherence to the underlying structure	To facilitate the asking of questions related to the overall process and specific points along the way	To assist the practitioner in navigating a coaching process by clarifying complexities	To facilitate new insights and planning for improved coaching effectiveness

Function 1—Organizing a Framework of Ideas about Coaching

The first function of a coaching model is to organize a framework of ideas about coaching. This framework of ideas ensures understanding of a particular approach to coaching by providing order and coherence to its underlying structure. An organizing framework enables you to think about and analyze how the elements of effective coaching relate to one another and to the larger purpose of coaching. When you have such a framework, you can clearly articulate and critically evaluate your approach to coaching.

To organize your coaching approach into a conceptual framework, you first identify and then select the essential components. What is fundamental to your approach to coaching? What do you consider to be the key factors? By selecting only the essential components, your model becomes accessible to you and to others. You can easily explain your approach. You can refer to it when you're stuck or when you want to identify where the person you are coaching is getting stuck. Paradoxically, keeping it simple will allow you to go deeper, to enhance your understanding by reflecting on each individual component of your coaching model.

Keep in mind that your coaching model is a work in progress. As you apply and reflect on your model, you may choose to modify it. As you increase your knowledge of coaching and evolve your coaching practice, your coaching model can evolve. As with any model, you can continue to refine it.

Examples of Coaching Frameworks

A cross-cultural business coach crafted a metaphor to describe how he organizes his concepts and knowledge about coaching. "I see myself as a pilot in a plane. The client is the co-pilot. We both face the same direction. We're both going somewhere. We're looking at and monitoring the same dials. The co-pilot chooses the destination. Rigorous ethics are the quality of the gasoline. Principles are the FAA (Federal Aviation Administration) regulations. Process involves pre-preparation, preparation for take-off, take-off, altitude rising, and cruising. On the dashboard, co-equals use the instruments and procedures. Addressing turbulence, resistance, and bumps along the way may be necessary."

A professional development coach works with a graphic model that she learned from the Newfield Network in its certified coach training program. It has three elements, OAR—the **O**bserver that we are; the **A**ctions that we take; and the **R**esults that we want to produce. People sometimes loop back and forth, caught between the same action and same result—the issue is with the Observer. Transformative change occurs when we start to see our actions and results differently, caused by a shift in the eye of the Observer.

The role as Observer is key and involves three dimensions: **B**ody, **E**motions/moods, and **L**anguage—referred to as the BEL components of the model. People are most coherent when these three dimensions are aligned (see Figure 4.1). The coherency—or lack of it—among the Body, Emotions/moods, and Language authentically reveals how that person shows up to himself or herself and to the public. Coherency among the three dimensions enables new learning, new habits, and enduring transformative change.

An executive coach derived her framework from the theories of Edward T. Hall, who proposed that culture and communication are reciprocal and interrelated. She focuses on the dimensions of relationship, communication, and time to help corporate executives think about and appreciate the importance of culture and context. Hall suggests that "understanding oneself and understanding others are closely related processes. To do one, you must start with the other, and vice

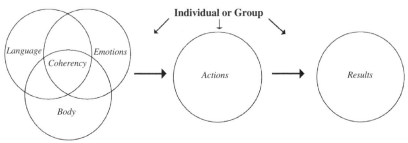

The observer that you are...   sees certain actions to take... to produce your desired results

Figure 4.1 The Newfield Network Coaching Model
© Newfield Network

versa" (1976, 69). She applies Hall's insights and concepts, such as framing, to specific problems faced in organizational settings. Hall describes situational frames as "the smallest viable unit of a culture that can be taught, transmitted and handed down as a complete entity. Frames contain linguistic, kinesic, proxemic, temporal, social, material, personality, and other components" (1976, 129).

Function 2—Highlighting the Key Elements of a Coaching Process
The second function of a coaching model is to highlight the key elements of a coaching process and their interrelationships. These elements facilitate the asking of questions within the context of an overall structure and specific points along the way. By highlighting aspects of the process, the coach becomes more aware of the big picture and key points from which to ask questions. The highlighted elements also help the coach deconstruct the coaching experience to solve problems and better understand the interactions.

To highlight the key elements, you need to identify the flow of your coaching process. What is most important to you at the beginning, middle, and end of the process? How do you approach what happens before, between, and after coaching interactions?

It is important to understand that a coaching model does not box you in or limit you in any way to a fixed, prescribed step-by-step process. Rather it highlights key points and features, allowing you to explore and reflect on your process, and incorporate new knowledge, skills, and practices. You can use your coaching model to expand your thinking about the many facets of the coaching process.

Examples of Key Elements Highlighted in the Coaching Process
A cross-cultural business coach's sequential process takes place over the course of a coaching engagement. He first builds a relationship; assesses

where the client is at present (often using a values instrument); and focuses on where the client is going and why (calling attention to the destination). The client reviews what has worked best (looking to the past, in particular contexts); sets goals (looking to the future); brainstorms (discussing how to get there); and selects strategies (and tactics). The coach then checks on balance (reaffirming that they are aligned and on the right track); and champions the client (acknowledging and celebrating the client's successes). When hired by a company to coach an executive, rather than hired directly by an individual, he provides the company with a plan of action that is worked out in advance by him and his client, a mid-term progress report, and a final progress report.

A leadership development coach refers to a model of *context–content–conduct* when she thinks about the flow of coaching. *Context* tasks may include: contracting and assessing; *content* tasks include giving feedback, exploring options, and planning for experimentation; and *conduct* tasks include experimenting, reflecting on learning, and executing.

An executive coach and consultant to organizations sees feedback as a process of conflict resolution and a stimulus for productive conversation. In his coaching practice, he enhances feedback opportunities. He provides a climate of support for clients to look at challenges they know exist but haven't been ready or able to confront. He chooses not to use 360-degree feedback, a formalized process in which employees receive confidential, anonymous feedback about a range of workplace competencies from the people with whom they work. His perspective on this common feedback collection practice is that the anonymous feedback survey forms become a way to avoid conflict and a substitute rather than a stimulus for conversation.

Instead of using the 360 instrument, he asks each client to give him the names of three people who have different perspectives on the behaviors the client wants to work on. Then, the coach lets the people being interviewed know his client is working on particular behaviors, interviews these people, and invites them to be resources for his client. He discusses the results of the interviews with the person he is coaching. He encourages the person not only to practice new behaviors, but also to follow with the people who gave feedback to make sure they recognize the new behaviors. This method increases opportunities for people in the organization to give and receive productive feedback to each other about important performance-related issues.

A coaching manager in a major pharmaceutical company, with experience as a sales representative, sales manager, and sales trainer, uses a coaching process that parallels the sales process. It begins with opening the discussion in ways that focus on the person's perception of what is needed and demonstrate the coach's commitment to supporting the person. She asks questions to discover the person's thought process, including beliefs, experiences, and goals. She discusses what it would mean to take a particular action—how it would add value or resolve a problem (a value proposition for the coaching process), then together they develop a plan. She closes a session by gaining agreement on next steps and a mutual exchange of commitments.

Function 3—Guiding Coaching Decisions and Actions

The third function of a coaching model is to guide coaching decisions and actions. A model assists you in navigating the coaching process by clarifying complexities. It helps you establish clearly defined guidelines for your coaching practice. It also focuses your attention on the fundamental aspects of coaching, enabling you to make informed decisions about your process and practice.

To guide coaching decisions and actions effectively, you must determine the nature of your coaching practice. Who will you coach . . . and who will you not? What issues will and won't you work on? When and why will you refer someone to another coach or other resources? What are you qualified to address . . . and what are you not? What are your beliefs about coaching and the underlying principles that guide your coaching interactions?

Your coaching model serves as a general guide, more like a compass than a road map. It is a device for determining your direction and monitoring your course. Whether your model is verbal or visual, it is a conceptual tool that enables you to think about your actions in coaching situations and your coaching practice in general.

Examples of the Model as a Guide for Coaching Decisions and Actions

A cross-cultural business coach differentiates coaching from mentoring, managing, consulting, counseling, teaching, psychotherapy, and friendship. He does this by articulating what each means to him, as well as what each means to a variety of subject matter experts. He also thinks about the importance of the coaching relationship and the boundaries between coach and client. He uses the term "dispassionate passion," meaning that the coach is passionate about the client's desires but stays separate, keeping clear boundaries.

He has a set of criteria for coaching excellence, including certain characteristics and personal qualities. Among these are: a results-orientation, caring, dependability, open-mindedness, firmness with flexibility, being a lifelong learner, walking the talk (that is, integrating values and actions), having integrity, and respecting boundaries. He believes in the importance of:

- Building trust—"implicitly, by manifesting reliability; and explicitly, by establishing and maintaining confidentiality."
- Listening, questioning, allowing silence, and championing the client.
- Asking for permission to coach, to suggest an agreement, or to give advice.
- Honoring agreements with his clients and not imposing any agreements on them.
- Coaching that is CLEAR: Client-centered (focusing on whatever the client wants); Life encompassing (bearing in mind the client's whole life); Equal (establishing and maintaining an egalitarian relationship between coach and client); Action-oriented (moving to goals and results); Realistic (designing goals that advance the client).

A coaching manager in a major pharmaceutical company coaches area sales managers, who, in turn, coach their territory managers. To have a common language, she and the sales managers as well as sales executives use a variety of tools that enable them to identify and describe behaviors that support the sales effort. One is a coaching form to record observations and evaluate seven key sales competencies. Each competency is tied to three or four observable traits; for example, the sales execution competency is associated with traits such as "can open a call with an agenda," and "can move with the customer's agenda." In addition to coaching reports and the DiSC personality assessment tool, she and other managers use the Gallup Organization's StrengthsFinder instrument to know when their strengths are useful, where to use them, and when they can cause problems. The managers provide coaching by building on positive strengths (as in the StrengthsFinder approach) to enhance the performance of their valued sales executives. This manager believes that:

- Coaching, in addition to training, makes change sustainable. "Without coaching, training becomes simply an event."
- Good salespeople and sales managers need to be recognized. "Their experiences need to be shared and trumpeted from the mountaintop."
- Coaching supports the sales force. "It makes them better—strong trees that will bend not break in the face of competitive pressures."

An executive coach and consultant to organizations gets to know his executive clients through conversations. The guiding principle of his coaching practice is that people can learn anything with support. To provide support, he needs to know a person's capability, capacity, and strengths; then he can know how best to stretch that person. He makes a clear distinction between providing assistance in terms of help and providing assistance in terms of support. "Help" is doing something *for* the other person, where the helper gets recognition and the person being helped may become dependent; "support" is learner-centered and stretches a person's capacity. This notion of support is central to his approach to coaching leaders. He places high value on assisting people to "find their voice, spread their wings, be supported, and put their best foot forward." He believes that:

- Leadership coaching often deals with conflict, defined as any incompatibility or opposition.
- Human social interaction is fraught with conflict that can be managed productively and a coach supports the client in dealing with conflict productively.
- Ongoing social situations at work have conflicts, but clients can learn to deal with the right people and the right issues; therefore they must identify the right issues and the right people.
- Being a good diagnostician (i.e. being able to understand a person's issue) comes with practice and experience. As he says about practice, "We're in no danger of finishing."
- If the coach is not learning, the clients are not learning.

Function 4—Serving as a Tool for Continual Learning by the Coach

The fourth function of a coaching model is to serve as a personalized tool for the coach's own continual learning, development, and performance. It facilitates new insights, discoveries, and planning for improved coaching effectiveness. The importance of this function of a coaching model cannot be overstated. By reflecting on your coaching model, you can pinpoint specific aspects of coaching to practice deliberately and improve.

What have you learned as a coach? What are you curious about? What skills and knowledge do you have about coaching? What do you need to learn more about or improve? To enhance your coaching capabilities and improve your effectiveness as a coach, it is necessary to identify and commit to self-development action plans. You can use the model to better understand yourself, your practice, your learning needs, and goals.

Excellent coaches are invariably continual learners. They seek ways to improve their skills and abilities and to increase their knowledge base. A clearly articulated, critically evaluated coaching model is a tool for reflecting on both your accomplishments and your limitations, as well as for gaining new insights and ways of thinking about coaching. It is a tool that can help you assess your development as a coach, identify specific areas for improvement, and plan for your continued learning.

Examples of Learning Strategies

A leadership development coach internalizes her model by practicing individual elements, thinking about ways to apply the model to coaching interactions, and reflecting on the model in terms of herself and her clients. She believes that knowledge of the model helps her understand the learning process that she goes through as the coach, not just her clients' process. She reflects in action and she reflects after action on what she noticed during her coaching experience. For additional learning, she talks with colleagues and mentor coaches, participates in learning groups and continuing education, reads, and reflects. She loves to learn.

An experienced business coach and educator expands her own boundaries by becoming the observer of herself. She reflects in action, works with a fellow coach, and uses all of her personal and professional experiences for learning.

A cross-cultural business coach reflects on his model. He engages in self-inquiry and continues his self-development by "reading promiscuously"—current affairs, economics, cross-cultural management, coaching, and fiction. He talks to people, sees films, and participates in several groups for coaches.

A professional development coach uses curiosity and reflection, which guide and feed each other. She finds that reflecting on her model can shine a light on what has been a blind spot. Her "ah-hah" moments come when she reflects after coaching. For additional learning, she enrolls in courses or programs, continues to practice Zen, including martial arts. She has a coach and is a firm believer in doing her own internal work with supervision.

An international executive coach emphasizes the importance of continual learning for coaches. "People who coach need to be lifelong learners or they become canned, stale or isolated."

CHARACTERISTICS OF USEFUL MODELS

Highly useful coaching models have certain characteristics in common:

- They are comprehensible, using plain language to make sense of and simplify complexities. Useful coaching models help you articulate what you do and why.

- They depict only the key factors, helping you think about what's important. Useful coaching models facilitate your learning process.
- They are frequently graphic, but not always. They can be visual or verbal. Useful coaching models do not imply closure but call attention to essentials to help you generate interesting questions and uncover new challenges.

By recognizing the framework of ideas that influence how you act and interact in coaching situations, you are in a position to question those ideas and make sure they are appropriate and constructive. Useful coaching models are tools for reflective practice. As Donald Schon suggests, reflective practice requires being curious and analytical about what you are doing and what effect it is likely to have (1983).

Useful coaching models enable you to reflect on your experiences—what you did, why, and what you might do in the future. What actually happened? Why do I think it happened in this way? What is my reaction to what happened? What would I do differently at another time? What will I do next? What have I learned? How, if at all, has this changed my ideas?

SUMMARY

Your coaching model illustrates your approach to coaching. The four central functions of the model are to:

1. Organize your ideas about coaching into a conceptual framework.
2. Highlight the key elements of your coaching process.
3. Guide your coaching decisions and actions.
4. Serve as a tool for your continual learning.

The model promotes understanding of a coaching approach by providing order and coherence to its underlying structure. It assists you in navigating a coaching process. In addition, it clarifies the complexities of coaching and facilitates new insights, as well as planning for your improved effectiveness as a coach. Coaching models are most useful when they are easy to understand, depict only key factors, either visually or verbally, and do not imply closure to the learning process.

Preceding chapters have included a review of the theoretical foundations of coaching models, theory-based guidelines for the process of model development, and some ways practitioners and managers have organized their framework of ideas about coaching. In the next chapter, you will find recommended strategies and reflective activities to assist you in identifying the key elements of your own coaching process. These strategies and activities will help clarify your coaching philosophy and core practices, including your preferred coaching methods and tools. They will facilitate your thinking about where you need to place boundaries around your coaching practice and where you can build on your unique combination of strengths. You will be preparing the groundwork and laying the foundation for your personalized coaching model.

5

IDENTIFICATION AND SELECTION OF COACHING MODEL COMPONENTS

This chapter lays the groundwork for developing and applying your own coaching model. First, it provides practical strategies for exploring your views about coaching. Then, it includes 16 reflective activities to help you identify perspectives, skills, knowledge, and experience that you can incorporate into your model. The strategies and activities presented in this chapter enable you to identify and select your model components; then you can organize them, either visually or verbally. As a result, you will have a personalized tool for reflecting on the essential elements of your coaching process and practice, and on your own effectiveness as a coach.

EXPLORING YOUR VIEWS ABOUT COACHING

How can you begin to identify the essential elements of your coaching process? How can you enhance your awareness of the influences on your coaching practice, and the knowledge, skills, and tools you can bring to coaching interactions? How can you continue learning about the key components of your coaching process and practice?

This section includes an investigation of the many ways that coaches and managers can heighten their awareness of the strengths they bring to the coaching process (see Figure 5.1).

Read about Coaching and Other Areas of Interest
An effective strategy for the development of a coaching model is to read books and articles about coaching approaches, principles, and

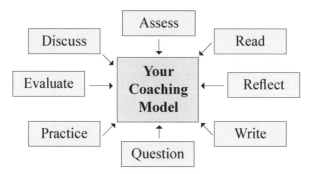

Figure 5.1 General Coaching Model Development Strategies

practices. As an example, *The CCL Handbook of Coaching: A Guide for the Leader Coach*, edited by Ting and Scisco, puts forth the leadership development model of the Center for Creative Leadership (CCL). This model consists of three parts:

1. *Relationship* as the context for coaching interactions;
2. *Assessment, challenge*, and *support* as the core elements of their leadership development model; and
3. *Results*.

In one chapter of the book, authors Sharon Ting and Doug Riddle note that CCL's view of coaching has evolved over 30 years of experience in developing individual leaders. It now recognizes the importance of collective leadership development, i.e. "creating and maintaining leadership capacity in and among groups, teams and organizations" (Ting and Riddle 2006, 61). Although CCL's views about the purposes and contexts of coaching evolve, leadership coaches continue to use the framework of essential elements (i.e. relationship, assessment, challenge, support, and results) as a guide for their decisions and actions.

The Coaching Manager by Hunt and Weintraub (2002) details a simple coaching model that can be incorporated into the daily routines of managers who want to help their employees learn and develop. *Coaching for Performance* by Whitmore (2004) details his coaching philosophy and GROW model, described briefly in Chapter 1 of this book. *Executive Coaching: Practices & Perspectives*, edited by Fitzgerald and Berger (2002), presents a variety of approaches and practices for coaching different audiences, including entrepreneurs, isolated executives, mid-life and senior executives. *Evidence Based Coaching Handbook*, edited by Stober and Grant (2006), describes many different coaching practices. Stober and Grant organize them by single-theory perspectives on coaching (e.g. cognitive coaching, behavior-based coaching) and integrative and cross-theory approaches (e.g. coaching from a systemic perspective, a contextual approach to coaching, adventure-based coaching). These books on coaching and many others are listed in the references section of this book.

You may also want to read books and articles that explore your areas of interest outside of coaching to gain insights or get new ideas about what to incorporate into your coaching model. For example, a part-time MBA student and project manager developed a coaching model informed by his reading and learning about Ken Blanchard's situational leadership model. Students have based their models on a wide range of sources, including: the principles of Martin Buber, a philosopher and theologian; experiences with a series of style and learning assessments; a study of wind-surfing methods. The list goes on. The more you read, the more you know and can draw on to enrich your coaching model.

Reflect, Write, and Discuss

Reflective activities invite you to recall experiences, construct meaning from information, investigate concepts, and analyze how the parts of a coaching process relate to each other and to a larger structure and purpose. You can learn a lot about your view of coaching by articulating your thoughts in writing. Reflective writing facilitates discovery, reveals your unique perspectives, and heightens awareness of your ways of thinking and acting. Writing allows you to describe and organize ideas in your own way. Additionally, you can discuss your thoughts with colleagues. By engaging in open, honest discussions with others, you can explore multiple perspectives, investigate your assumptions, hypothesize, problem-solve, and bring together diverse ideas into a coherent whole. Later in this chapter, a series of reflective activities are presented. They are designed for you to do alone, with a colleague, or both.

Assess Your Style and Communication Skills

There are various self-assessment tools you can use to gain insights about your style, skills, and preferences. Among the personal style assessments, you can select instruments that focus on your learning style, team member style, leadership style, or personality style. Describing individual differences and behavioral preferences dates back as far as 400 BC when the Greek physician Hippocrates named four temperaments after human body fluids he believed influenced the personality. The first is the melancholic type, described as fact-oriented and intellectual. The second is the sanguine type, described as action-oriented and social/emotional. The third is the choleric type, described as ideals-oriented and dominant. The fourth is the phlegmatic type, described as theory-oriented and neutral.

In the 1920s, Swiss psychologist Carl Jung identified four styles based on preferred mental functioning. Some people prefer to perceive information through sensing and others prefer intuiting; and some prefer to make judgments through thinking and others prefer feeling. In 1958, psychologist Isabel Myers and her mother Katheryn Briggs expanded on Jung's type formula and developed the Myers-Briggs Type Inventory (MBTI). This tool is commonly used in corporations for improving management, teambuilding, leadership development, and communication. The 16 MBTI types assess your orientation (introvert-**I** or extrovert-**E**); preferences for information intake (sensing-**S** or intuiting-**N**) and method of decision-making (thinking-**T** or feeling-**F**); and primary and auxiliary functions used in the outer world (judging-**J** or perceiving-**P**).

DiSC, an acronym for *dominance, influence, steadiness, compliance*, is a commonly used typology of behavioral styles and preferences. The model was developed by John Geier, based on the behavioral studies of Harvard psychologist William Moulton Marston in 1928. The studies revealed four primary behavioral styles with distinct patterns of observable behavior. From this, the DiSC assessment tool was created to help people better understand themselves and others. It is used for personal and professional development in a variety of organizational contexts.

A word of caution is necessary here. Assessments are best viewed as tools to increase self-awareness. They are not intended to be used as labels. Styles are simply a preference and a choice, not what you are. It is important to recognize and appreciate that you can access all these styles and continually expand the range of your behaviors. You have skills and abilities from all styles.

Other questionnaires are designed to provide insights about your communication skills. Examining your listening and questioning skills, for example, is essential for every coach, regardless of your approach, context, or target audience. A simple listening assessment will show you where you have strengths and where you can improve. Coaching self-inventories, such as the one created by Dennis Kinlaw, are particularly useful for people who have had some previous experience coaching. Kinlaw's coaching self-inventory differentiates the skills used in performing five "coaching functions":

1. *contact and core communication* skills to initiate coaching

conversations, demonstrate respect, and establish openness to others' views;

2. *counseling* skills to help people find their own solutions to problems;

3. *mentoring* skills to develop in others political savvy, awareness of organizational culture, and career development opportunities;

4. *tutoring* skills to help others gain knowledge and the expertise they need for their work; and

5. *confronting and challenging* skills to help others achieve superior performance (1999).

Although Kinlaw's distinctions may be different from your own, you benefit from identifying strengths in your skill set, along with areas for development.

Practice and Reflect

In addition to using the communication skills of coaching and reflecting on them, consider making a commitment to developing specific strategies for improving your skills and abilities through "deliberate practice." In his excellent and important book, *Talent is Overrated*, Geoff Colvin examines world-class performance and advances the concept of deliberate practice (2008).

Based on research studies, particularly those of Anders Ericsson and his colleagues, deliberate practice is characterized as:

> activity designed specifically to improve performance, often with a teacher's help; it can be repeated a lot; feedback on results is continuously available; it is demanding mentally, whether the activity is purely intellectual, such as chess or business-related activities, or heavily physical, such as sports; and it isn't much fun (Colvin 2008, 66).

An important skill for developing superior performance is the ability to identify the particular elements of performance—skills and abilities—that need to be improved. If you are committed to stretching far beyond your current level of ability, consider learning about and engaging in deliberate practice.

Evaluate Your Interactions

You can easily collect feedback about your communication behavior and coaching effectiveness. Ask the people with whom you communicate and coach for feedback. If you don't ask, you might not know the impact your behavior is having on others or whether what you do and say are effective—or not. Use relatively open-ended questions so you can get the most information and encourage people to say whatever is on their minds. *How useful has the coaching been for you? What did I do or say that was most helpful? What was least helpful? Any suggestions? Any problems? Any other feedback you want to give me?* You will be able to gather information and evaluate the effectiveness of your coaching interactions by asking simple, short, open-ended questions, e.g. *How was that?*

Question Yourself and Others

Knowledge is produced in response to questions, and new knowledge results from the asking of questions; quite often new questions about old questions . . . Once you have learned how to ask questions—relevant and appropriate and substantial questions— you have learned how to learn and no one can keep you from learning whatever you want or need to know (Postman and Weingartner 1969, 23).

Inquiry can take many forms. Peter Senge writes about inquiry as "holding conversations where we openly share views and develop knowledge about each other's assumptions" (1994, 237). He promotes the practice of balancing advocacy and inquiry. This involves stating your views and how you came to them, then encouraging others to think with you about your ideas. Not only is it important to express your views, it is important to hear and consider the multiple perspectives of others. In a dialogue, it is a useful practice to put forward your position. Then ask if it makes sense to others and if they can see ways to improve on it. The key to balancing advocacy and inquiry is to make your own reasoning explicit and remain open and curious about the ways others view what you've said. This reflective thinking requires practice but is well worth the investment. Through inquiry with others, you can gain insights into what you think about coaching and why, what you don't yet know and understand, and what others know and understand that may be different from your perspective.

REFLECTIVE ACTIVITIES

This section includes 16 reflective activities designed to facilitate a process of inner search, self-dialogue, and self-discovery (see Figure 5.2). As a result of completing these activities, you will become more aware of the lenses through which you view coaching. The questions posed

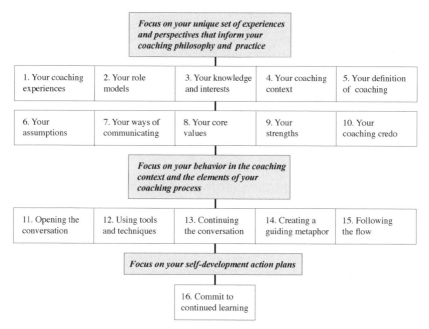

Figure 5.2 Reflective Activities to Increase Awareness of Your Coaching Orientation

in these activities strengthen your ability to clarify your coaching orientation and identify essential elements of your coaching process.

Reflective activities 1–10 focus on your unique set of experiences and perspectives that inform your coaching philosophy and practice. Reflective activities 11–15 focus on your behavior in the coaching context and the elements of your coaching process. Reflective activity 16 relates to your development as a coach.

How To Use These Reflective Activities

1. Make sure you do not use these activities as a rigid, step-by-step recipe for building a model. They are designed to increase your awareness about your coaching orientation and to help you identify important elements of your coaching process and practice. It is up to you to select the essential components of your model and then to frame them, visually or verbally, in a way that has the most meaning and relevance for you.

2. Make sure you do each activity in sequence. The series of activities focuses first on your background and beliefs about coaching, then on your coaching behaviors. You will find key questions in each activity to help guide your thought process. Whether you are a student of coaching, an experienced practitioner, or a manager who coaches employees, you will benefit from doing the task and responding to the questions in each of the reflective activities.

Reflective Activity 1	Describe your coaching experience
Purpose: To discover your mental model of coaching *Result:* Identification of some of the essential elements of your approach to coaching *Reference:* Chapter 3 Guidelines: Experience—use your personal and professional experiences as a resource; *Analyze your participation*	**Background** Your coaching experiences—when you coached or were coached—shape your beliefs about coaching and your approach to coaching. Recalling specific information about these experiences and describing the coaching outcomes helps you become aware of your existing mental model, or internal picture, of how coaching works as a system. **Task** Recall a particular time when you coached someone or received coaching at work or school. • When and where did the coaching take place? • Who was instrumental in making it happen? • What happened during the coaching experience and what were the outcomes? • What insights did you gain as a result of this coaching experience? **Application to Coaching Model Development** After doing this activity, what have you learned about your mental model of coaching?

Reflective Activity 2	Describe a role model
Purpose: To discover characteristics and behaviors of coaching that impact you positively *Result:* Identification of what matters to you as a coach *Reference:* Chapter 3 Guidelines: Experience—use your personal and professional experiences as a resource; *Analyze your social connections*	**Background** Role models are people whose behavior in a particular role is imitated by others. Your role models for coaching have certain qualities and skills that you respect and admire. They perform desired behaviors. An analysis of the characteristics and behaviors of your role models provides valuable learning about people who have a positive impact on others. **Task** Recall a particular time when you interacted with a coaching role model. • How would you describe this person's qualities? • What actions did this person take? • How did this person's actions make you feel? • How did this person affect your thinking, decisions, and actions? **Application to Coaching Model Development** After doing this activity, what have you learned about characteristics and behaviors you value and want to bring to coaching interactions?

Reflective Activity 3   Deepen your knowledge

Purpose:
To reflect on your areas of interest and expertise

Result:
Awareness of the relevance of multiple disciplines and knowledge domains to your approach to coaching

Reference:
Chapter 3 Guidelines: Experience—use your personal and professional experiences as a resource; *Analyze your interests and expertise*

Background
Particular domains capture your interest and stimulate you intellectually. By deepening your conceptual knowledge (theories and structures) and procedural knowledge (skills and methods), you build rich mental models of these domains. These knowledge domains can inform the ways you think about and frame your approach to coaching.

Task
List the knowledge domains that interest you and that you intend to continue to explore. (As you read earlier, coaches have drawn on sports, psychology, science, and a wide variety of other interests to shape their approach to coaching.)

- What are some of the key components (e.g. principles, practices, elements, paradigms) of these domains?
- How do these components relate to coaching?
- What are some ways to gain more conceptual and procedural knowledge of these domains?
- What action step(s) will you commit to taking that will deepen your knowledge?

Application to Coaching Model Development
After doing this activity, what have you learned about how these knowledge domains can enrich the ways you think about and frame your approach to coaching?

Reflective Activity 4	**Envision the context**
Purpose: To generate a list of images that describe your perspectives about the context of coaching *Result:* Creation of a personally relevant image of your desired coaching context *Reference:* Chapter 3 Guidelines: Experience—use your personal and professional experiences as a resource; *Analyze the communication contexts*	**Background** You can think about the context of coaching, i.e. the setting in which coaching takes place, in metaphorical terms. Metaphors and analogies can be used to describe things. They suggest some likeness between two seemingly unlike objects or ideas. These figures of speech can provide you with memorable visual images. (As you read in previous chapters, coaches have described their process as conversation, a sports game and other metaphors.) **Task** Use metaphors or analogies to describe the context of coaching. Complete the sentence, "The coaching context is like . . ." or "The coaching context is . . ." List as many metaphorical expressions as you can without editing yourself. • What do you notice about your list? • What commonalities can you identify? • What aspects of these images do you find compelling? • Why are these aspects important to you? **Application to Coaching Model Development** After doing this activity, what have you learned about the coaching context you want to create and provide?

Before you start the next activity, read these practitioners' definitions of coaching.

Gallwey's formula to describe his approach:

Performance = potential − interference (2001, 17).

Whitmore's definition of coaching:

> Coaching is not merely a technique to be wheeled out and rigidly applied in certain prescribed circumstances. It is a way of managing, a way of treating people, a way of thinking, a way of being (2004, 18).

O'Neill's description of coaching:

> The essence of coaching is helping leaders get unstuck from their dilemmas and assisting them in transferring their learning into results for the organization (2000, xiii).

Peltier's views about executive coaching:

> Someone from outside an organization uses psychological skills to help a person develop into a more effective leader. These skills are applied to specific present-moment work problems in a way that enables this person to incorporate them into his or her permanent management or leadership repertoire (2001, xx).

Hunt and Weintraub's conception of developmental coaching:

> Developmental coaching is a helping relationship between a manager, and most often, his or her employees (though coaching managers may coach others in their organization); its goal is the growth and development of employees (2002, xiii).

Zeus and Skiffington's description of a coach:

> An expert in the use of behavioral change tools and techniques (2002, 6).

Renwick's roles during coaching interactions:

> Quiet explorer, creative colleague, client-centered tutor, seasoned advisor (2006).

Silsbee's septet coaching model roles:

> Master, partner, investigator, reflector, teacher, guide and contractor (2004).

Reflective Activity 5   Define coaching

Purpose: To synthesize your discoveries and insights about coaching from Reflective Activities 1–4. *Result:* Creation of a personally relevant definition of coaching *Reference:* Chapter 3 Guidelines: Experience—use your personal and professional experiences as a resource	**Background** Coaching is not therapy, consulting, or mentoring. Although there are some similarities among them, there are also significant differences. It is important for you to reflect on the boundaries, as well as the structure, of your coaching practice. *"Top business coaches are as clear about what they don't do as about what they can deliver"* (Scoular 2009, 31). **Task** Articulate the way you view the practice of coaching. Complete the sentence, "Coaching is . . ." Use your own words to frame the way you see coaching. • Review your responses to Reflective Activities 1–4. • Write or discuss your definition of coaching with a colleague. • Be aware that you can modify your definition of coaching as you develop and apply your own coaching model.

Reflective Activity 6   Examine your assumptions

Purpose:
To identify assumptions you take for granted about people and learning

Result:
Heighten your awareness of assumptions that inform your behavior in a coaching context

Reference:
Chapter 3 Guidelines: Reflection—act and reflect to continue the learning process; *Analyze your cultural background*

Keep in mind that a cultural group might include your family, occupation, organization, etc. Each of these groups has key assumptions about people and learning that may, or may not, influence your coaching approach.

Background
"Culture is a pattern of shared basic assumptions that was learned by a group as it solved its problems of external adaptation and internal integration, that has worked well enough to be considered valid and, therefore, to be taught to new members as the correct way to perceive, think, and feel in relation to those problems" (Schein 2004, 17).

Members of groups share, to varying degrees, cultural frames of reference. Shared learning experiences lead to shared assumptions. Cultural understanding involves becoming aware of taken-for-granted assumptions that underlie behavior.

Task
Think about the cultural groups to which you belong and with which you identify. Draw 3 columns on a piece of paper. In the left column, list the groups that you belong to in priority order—from the most to the least important to you now. In the middle column, list 2 or 3 of each group's key assumptions about people and learning. Leave the column on the right blank until the next activity.
• What do you notice about your list of cultural group memberships and their assumptions?
• Which of these assumptions do you (and don't you) share?
• What insights did you gain about yourself?
• How do these insights relate to your approach to coaching?

Application to Coaching Model Development
What have you learned from your assumptions that inform your behavior in a coaching context?

Reflective Activity 7	Examine communication behavior norms
Purpose: To identify cultural norms (common and generally accepted patterns) of communication behavior *Result:* Selection of communication behaviors essential to your coaching practice *Reference:* Chapter 3 Guidelines: Reflection—act and reflect to continue the learning process; *Analyze communication behavior norms* Shared and accepted ways of communicating are "norms of communication behavior."	**Background** Culture influences your ways of communicating. Consider the ways of communicating that you share with members of the groups to which you belong and with which you identify (the same groups you listed in the previous activity). **Task** Think about the ways each cultural group to which you belong communicates. Take the 3-column chart you created in the previous activity. To complete the column on the right, list 2 or 3 of each group's norms of communication behavior. For example, a communication norm might be to bring up problems only when you have a solution. • What do you notice about your list of cultural norms of communication behavior? • Which of these norms of communication behavior do you (and don't you) share? • What insights did you gain about yourself? • How do these insights relate to your approach to coaching? **Application to Coaching Model Development** What have you learned about the communication behaviors you want to bring to coaching?

Reflective Activity 8   Clarify your core values

Purpose:
To identify core values that guide
your behavior

Result:
Clarification of values that drive your behavior in the coaching context

Reference:
Chapter 3 Guidelines: Reflection—act and reflect to continue the learning process; *Analyze your core values and beliefs*

Some examples of values: achievement, authenticity, awareness, caring, challenge, change, choice, collaboration, competition, curiosity, empathy, flexibility, freedom, fun, honesty, integrity, learning, openness, productivity, relationships, resourcefulness, respect, responsibility, results, success, trust.

Background
Your personal values are principles that you consider to be intrinsically or extrinsically desirable. In the coaching context, strongly held values guide your behavior. Your values influence not only the selection of your methods but the ends you desire. In short, your core values inform your coaching orientation.

Task
To clarify what you most value, consider:
• What are the five values that are most important to you?
• What values do you want to express more fully?
• How do these values guide your everyday actions and decisions?
• How do these values inform your coaching choices and your view of what makes coaching effective?

Application to Coaching Model Development
What have you learned about your core values that can enhance the impact and effectiveness of your coaching process and practice?

Reflective Activity 9	Build on your strengths

Purpose: Identify your strengths *Result:* Awareness of strengths that are essential to your coaching process and practice *Reference:* Chapter 3 Guidelines: Reflection—act and reflect to continue the learning process; *Analyze your individual traits*	**Background** Focus on your strengths. These are assets you can leverage and refine. Becoming aware of your strengths and further developing them will improve your coaching performance. **Task** Write a brief description of yourself in the third person. Describe when you helped a friend, family member, or colleague successfully resolve a personal or professional problem. Emphasize your strengths. • How have your strengths served you? • How could your strengths in excess become liabilities? • How can you apply your strengths in a coaching context? • What actions can you take to further develop your strengths? **Application to Coaching Model Development** What have you learned about how your strengths are demonstrated in your coaching process and practice?

Before you start the next activity, read about these practitioners' coaching beliefs.

Hunt and Weintraub's basic beliefs about the coaching manager's "coaching mind-set":

Coaching managers don't believe in the "sink or swim" theory of employee development . . . Coaching managers believe that by helping their employees develop, everybody comes out ahead (2002, 43).

O'Neill's basic belief about leaders and executive coaching "with backbone and heart":

> There is a value embedded in the method. It is the belief that leaders have within them most of the resources they need to address the very issues that seem most daunting (2000, 12).

Gallwey's basic belief about learning and coaching:

> The simple principles and methods of the Inner Game were based on a profound trust in the student's natural capability to learn from direct experience (2001, xxii).

Whitmore's basic belief about the potential within each person being coached:

> Unless the manager or coach believes that people possess more capability than they are currently expressing, he will not be able to help them express it. He must think of his people in terms of their potential, not their performance (2004, 13).

Zeus and Skiffington's basic beliefs about coaching and organizational change:

> Change is at the heart of coaching. Coaching plays a critical role in helping individuals and organizations create, adapt to and accept change as a challenge rather than an obstacle. The process can be a difficult one though (2002, 25).

Peltier writes about Carl Rogers' person-centered approach and humanistic beliefs:

> A consistent theme underlies most of Rogers' writing: deep faith in the tendency of people to develop in a positive and constructive manner if a climate of respect and trust is established (2001, 69).

Reflective Activity 10   Write your coaching credo

Purpose: To synthesize your discoveries and insights about coaching from Reflective Activities 5–9	**Background** Your coaching credo is a set of your beliefs that guide your actions in a coaching context. To know your beliefs requires self-examination and focused thought. It is important to do this because your beliefs shape the ways in which you see coaching and frame your practice.
Result: Creation of a personally relevant coaching credo	
Reference: Chapter 3 Guidelines: Reflection—act and reflect to continue the learning process	**Task** Determine what you believe about coaching and write your personal coaching philosophy. Consider the beliefs you hold about people and learning that might dispose you to act or react in certain ways (e.g. "People can change" . . . "People have choices" . . . "Learners know best how they learn" . . . "Learners respond to respect"). Include your most important beliefs about coaching.

Reflective Activity 11   Open the conversation

Purpose: To identify ways to set the context in which a productive coaching conversation can unfold	**Background** The opening of a coaching conversation sets the tone and significantly influences what follows. It is important to know what conditions you consider essential and what you want to establish up front.
Result: Selection of steps critical to building a foundation for your coaching conversations	**Task** Choose a situation that requires a conversation with someone to better understand a work-related issue. Conduct the conversation and then reflect on it. • What did you say and do to open the conversation? • What was your intention when you made those action choices? • What happened as a result? • What else could you say and do in the opening to create the conditions for a productive interaction?
	Application to Coaching Model Development What have you learned about the conditions you want to set and the ways in which you want to open a coaching conversation?

Reflective Activity 12	Think about tools and techniques
Purpose: To explore possible tools and techniques that can be a springboard for coaching conversations **Result:** Knowledge of tools and techniques that can enhance your coaching interactions Examples: Tools for working with mental models include the "ladder of inference" (described in Chapter 3); and the "left-hand column exercise" (based on the two-column research method developed by Argyris and Schon, 1974) where you write (in the right-hand column) what was actually said during a difficult conversation, then write (in the left-hand column) what you were thinking and feeling but not saying	**Background** Tools are instruments you can use to enhance your coaching interactions. Techniques are the ways in which the tools are used. **Task** Review the following list of tools. Do a search then go to the websites of one or two of the tools listed below that interest you: Belbin Team Inventory; Birkman Method; DISC Profile Tests; Enneagram Personality Type Indicator; EQ In-Action Profile: FIRO-B; Kolb Learning Style Inventory; Myers-Briggs Type Indicator; Personal Interests, Attitudes and Values Profile; 360 BY DESIGN. • What information did you gather about these tools from their websites? • What are some ways to use these tools? • What value could they add to your coaching? • What tools and techniques do you think would work best/least for you and why? **Application to Coaching Model Development** What have you learned about the role of tools and their relevance to your coaching process?

Reflective Activity 13   Continue the conversation

Purpose:
To identify the roles and behaviors of a coach during a coaching interaction

Result:
Awareness of roles and behaviors that further your coaching conversations

Background
The continuation of a coaching conversation requires the coach to think and act flexibly. Coaches must be able to adjust to the diverse needs, styles and responses of the people they coach to the coaching process. In addition to cognitive and behavioral flexibility, coaching demands authentic openness on the part of the coach to facilitate the learning process.

Task
Choose a situation that requires a conversation with someone to understand a work-related issue better. Conduct the conversation and then reflect on it.
- What did you say and do to continue the conversation?
- What roles did you take?
- What happened as a result?
- What are your preferred methods, or sequence of actions, to facilitate the learning of the person being coached during the conversation?

Application to Coaching Model Development
What have you learned about the roles and actions you choose to take to move the coaching process forward?

Reflective Activity 14	Develop a metaphor for the coaching process

Purpose: To generate an image that describes the flow of your coaching interactions *Result:* Creation of a personally relevant image of your coaching process	**Background** A process is "a progressive forward movement from one point to another on the way to completion: continued onward movement" (Merriam-Webster's Unabridged Dictionary). When you describe the coaching process by using a visual metaphor, you can achieve breakthroughs in thinking. The metaphor can weave together your memories, experiences, knowledge, skills, and beliefs. Because you choose a visual image that resonates and rings true for you, the metaphor respects your own interpretation and way of representing the coaching process. **Task** Think of a visual metaphor to describe the coaching process. Draw the picture that pops into your mind. • What are the elements of this image and how are the elements connected? • How does this image relate to the coaching process? • What could you add? • What new insights have you gained? **Application to Coaching Model Development** What have you learned about the flow of your coaching process?

Before you start the next activity, read about these practitioners' coaching processes.

Gallwey's Inner Game model:

He asks descriptive, non-judgmental questions, eliminating the interference of unhelpful beliefs (self-talk) and generating non-judgmental awareness and focused attention (2001).

Whitmore's GROW model:

It is based on a structured series of open-ended questions that establish, examine and explore Goals, Reality of the current situation, Options or action strategies to accomplish the goals, and Will or what the client will do (2004).

Hunt and Weintraub's developmental coaching process:

It begins with the manager identifying learning opportunities (coaching moments), then stopping the action and starting the coaching dialogue with questions to encourage reflection. Next, the coaching manager serves as a mirror by observing relevant actions and providing helpful, balanced feedback. It ends with the manager working together with the employee being coached to understand what needs to change, setting a goal for change and then following up (2002).

Zeus and Skiffington's team coaching process:

Team coaches work with the leader and members of a team to establish the mission, vision, strategy, and operating procedures of the team members with one another—a six-step process that involves working with members of a team over a period of several weeks or months (2002).

O'Neill's executive coaching model:

She grounds her coaching approach in systems theory and action research, an orientation to inquiry used in the organizational development field (2000).

Kemp's adventure-based coaching model:

He integrates David Kolb's experiential learning cycle, a process in which the learner makes sense of concrete experiences, with adventure programming, the intentional use of adventure experiences (such as wilderness expeditions or a ropes course) to create learning in individuals and groups. The first phase begins with the coach explaining the adventure metaphor and how it applies to the coaching context (2006).

Reflective Activity 15   Focus on the flow

Purpose:
To synthesize your discoveries and insights about coaching from Reflective Activities 11–14

Result:
Articulation of the flow of your coaching process

Definition of coaching process used in this book: the flow of coaching from preparing and opening to continuing and closing

Background
Coaching conversations can be brief or extended. They can be informal or formal. They can occur regularly on a set schedule or they can occur when a particular circumstance arises. But there is a flow to each coaching conversation—it opens, proceeds and closes.

Task
Articulate the way you view your coaching process. Consider your preferred methods, tools and the flow of your conversations.
- Review your responses to Reflective Activities 11–14.
- Write about or discuss your coaching process with a colleague.
- Keep in mind that you can modify your coaching process as you develop and apply your own coaching model.

Reflective Activity 16   Commit to continued learning

Purpose: To plan for continued learning as you develop and apply your coaching model *Result:* Creation of an action plan for developing as a coach and improving your coaching effectiveness The strategies for developing your coaching model described in this chapter include: *Read about coaching and other areas of interest; Reflect, write, and discuss; Assess your style and communication skills; Practice and reflect; Evaluate your interactions; Question yourself and others*	**Background** Review the strategies for developing your coaching model suggested in this chapter. As you develop and refine your coaching model, use these same strategies to continue your learning and development as a coach. **Task** Specify action steps for your continuous learning. Complete the sentences below to generate a self-development action plan. • I will discuss . . . • I will assess . . . • I will read . . . • I will reflect . . . • I will write . . . • I will question . . . • I will practice . . . • I will evaluate . . . Write or discuss this with a colleague. Make this a regular practice. Keep a journal to record your action commitments.

SUMMARY

Explore your views about coaching.

- *Read* about coaching and other areas of interest.
- *Reflect, write,* and *discuss.*
- *Assess* your style and communication skills.
- *Practice* and *reflect.*
- *Evaluate* your interactions.
- *Question* yourself and others.

Complete Reflective Activities 1–15, which focus on your background, beliefs, and behavior in a coaching context.

- RA 1: Describe your coaching experience.
- RA 2: Describe a role model.
- RA 3: Deepen your knowledge.
- RA 4: Envision the context.
- RA 5: Define coaching.
- RA 6: Examine your assumptions.
- RA 7: Examine communication behavior norms.
- RA 8: Clarify your core values.
- RP 9: Build on your strengths.
- RA 10: Write your coaching credo.
- RA 11: Open the conversation.
- RA 12: Think about tools and techniques.
- RA 13: Continue the conversation.
- RA 14: Develop a metaphor for the coaching process.
- RA 15: Focus on the flow.

Create an action plan to continue your learning and development as a coach.

- RA 16: Commit to continued learning.

In Part II of this book, you have reviewed some coaching models developed by practitioners and corporate managers, and have focused on the development of your own coaching model. In Part III, you will see how I developed my own coaching model. This first-hand demonstration of coaching model development and application begins in the next chapter with an explanation of how one particular coaching model evolved.

Part III
The Performance Coaching Model Example

6

HOW THE PERFORMANCE COACHING
MODEL EVOLVED

The third and final part of *Coaching Models: A Cultural Perspective* describes the evolution of the author's own coaching model, the Performance Coaching Model. It illustrates how one coach incorporates unique perspectives and sets of skills, knowledge, and experience into a coaching practice.

To show how one coaching model evolved, this chapter focuses on the coach's background, beliefs, and behaviors in a coaching context. It first discusses the coach's experiences that led to the development of the model. It then discusses some of the coach's perspectives and underlying principles of the model. It ends with a description of the process orientation and structure of the coaching sessions.

BACKGROUND

The development of the Performance Coaching Model was influenced by the theories and practices discussed throughout this book. As you read the details of how this one particular approach to coaching evolved, keep in mind that you can incorporate your unique set of personal and professional experiences and unique set of perspectives into your own coaching model (see Table 6.1).

Seeing Through the Theatre Lens

How did my life story—my unique set of experiences and perspectives —shape my approach to coaching? To trace the development of the coaching model I have used with corporate executives, business

Table 6.1
Individual Cultural Orientation

Unique Set of Experiences	Unique Set of Perspectives
• **Participation** Meaningful personal and professional experiences	• **Cultural Background** Group memberships that influence your sense of identity, e.g. discipline, industry, education, organization, geography, family of origin
• **Social Connections** Key contacts who influence your ways of thinking and acting	• **Communication Behavior Norms** Forms and norms of communication behavior
• **Interests and Expertise** Major interests and areas of expertise	• **Core Values and Beliefs** Guiding principles, core values, and beliefs
• **Contexts** Settings in which your communication takes place	• **Individual Traits** Personal style, qualities, competencies, strengths

students, and educators, I must start at an early point in my life. For as long as I can remember, my activities have revolved around learning and the performing arts. As a child, I spent most of my free time either doing schoolwork and studying or taking ballet classes and practicing for dance recitals. From age 6 through 12, I studied in a rigorous ballet school program with the Metropolitan Opera Ballet Company. After the first two years of intensive training, I performed as a dancer in opera productions on the stage of the magnificent, old Metropolitan Opera House. It was a grand experience.

Performing for an audience of almost 4,000 people each night had a big impact on me. I began to learn about creating a relationship with audience members, establishing connection, and then having communication occur based on what is intended, extended, and received. I started to understand that this connection with audience occurs in the middle, where the communication happens—not inside oneself or in the audience reaction, but in the "in-between." There is a meeting of the giver and receiver; both presenter and audience member are in a reciprocal relationship.

This moment of connection cannot happen by the presenter's actions alone. It requires meeting with another, meeting with what is present, being present to another individual or group. The definition of the word "audience," which comes from "to hear"—audire, audientia—involves:

- the act of hearing or attention to that which is heard, usually words
- a formal hearing, an opportunity of being heard
- a listener or assembly of listeners.

From a young age, I became aware that when we are present to another we become an audience—and that being heard matters.

In my teens, I became interested in expanding my world and exploring new areas of study. Moving away from a singular focus on the formal tradition of ballet, I studied modern dance and learned to play the piano. An open-minded piano teacher supported my interest in exploring different genres of music, from classical to folk music. The many ways that individuals and cultural groups express their thoughts and feelings musically fascinated me. I soon discovered an interest in learning about different cultures and the joy of singing and accompanying myself on the piano. I auditioned and was accepted as a vocal music major at the High School of Music and Art in New York City. Not only did this specialized public school offer an excellent academic program, it afforded me the opportunity to spend half of every school day studying and practicing music. As a vocal music major, I was required to learn and perform Italian arias, German lieder, and French art songs. I received voice training every day at school and supplemented this with private lessons outside of school. It became clear to me that making a commitment to disciplined, deliberate practice was necessary for achieving excellent performance.

Unfortunately, singing operatic music held no personal meaning for me. My voice was not expressing my own thoughts and feelings. To counter this, I joined a repertory theatre company. I spent afternoons, evenings, and weekends studying acting, theatre history, and different performance styles from around the globe. I rehearsed and performed plays in New York City theatres with a group of talented young performers and a dedicated acting teacher from Cuba, named Jack Romano. Throughout my high school years, I devoted a great deal of time and energy to this theatre group. It became the central focus of my everyday life.

I immersed myself in the study of different forms of theatre and dance in cultures around the world. I enthusiastically participated in creative projects, collaborating with my peers. And I was energized by the group's passionate interest in the theatre. I experienced a deep level of trust with people who shared a common interest in the arts. During and after college, I performed professionally at theatres around the country, taught acting, and directed plays at schools and international leadership programs. Throughout this period, I followed related interests. I continued to learn and practice techniques for using my body and voice to express ideas, expanding my range and enhancing my ability to respond flexibly to improvisational training activities.

After graduating from college and while studying for my master's degree in education, I developed a system in which I taught acting techniques to groups of people. I then formed these groups into theatre companies that created and performed their own original productions. The combination of studying and performing gave the participants an opportunity to practice skills, apply what they had learned, and express their own ideas to audiences in actual performance settings. Special emphasis was placed on having the students first learn technique and practice, then develop original material and prepare for performance.

It was extremely satisfying and rewarding to teach acting techniques to diverse groups of people in the United States and Europe, then direct and produce their original theatre productions. I felt privileged to be a facilitator of their learning, creating the conditions for people of various ages and backgrounds to find their voices and express themselves in a public setting. By weaving their stories into theatrical productions that became public events, their unique voices were heard.

Seeing Business through the Theatre Lens

When my personal circumstances changed, I committed to a new course of action. I entered the arena of for-profit business, taking a job in a media company. I discovered that my theatre training could guide me through each new encounter and enable me to grow and develop professionally. Not only did I discover that my ability to communicate with diverse audiences was an asset and a skill, I realized that I could rely on my knowledge and improvisational theatre techniques to assist me in learning from new situations. I undertook new projects, created new opportunities, and accepted the challenge of continuously improving my performance.

I entered the world of media and advertising by creating a role for myself as a developer of new business for a magazine. It was the first of several jobs that I created where none had existed before, another indirect influence from my previous work in the arts. After seeing this pattern repeated several times, I learned that it was not only easier but much more satisfying for me to create new job descriptions and then fill them than to attempt to fit into existing ones. I had to learn as I went along. I relied on the practiced skills of listening and communicating with diverse audiences. I also drew on my past experience working with a trusted group. These past skills and experience helped me to become a brand marketing and communication specialist for multinational corporate clients in the global media and entertainment industry.

I applied the metaphor of theatre to each new business challenge. For example, I developed brand identities as if I were creating a character in a play. I developed strategic marketing plans as if I were envisioning how I would direct a play. I created integrated marketing communication programs as if I were engaging in virtual dialogues with diverse audiences. I strategically positioned clients in the competitive global marketplace as if I were blocking scenes with many characters, all on the stage at the same time. I approached client meetings as if I were doing improvisations with other actors. In short, I applied the principles and practices of acting and improvisation to specific work situations and to develop business skills.

This phase of my life was filled with the challenge of entering new domains of activity and new client organizations, working in new corporate and country cultures, interacting with diverse teams, and handling diverse types of assignments. Looking back, I recognize how much I relied on my knowledge and skills of acting, improvisation, and performance to work creatively and effectively in ambiguous, often complex, and unfamiliar situations. My previous training in the performing arts had become an invaluable tool for me in the domain of business. It enabled me to move from client to client, project to project. In addition, it made it possible for me to approach new situations in a way that allowed me to continue to learn, practice, and grow personally and professionally.

I worked for several years as the brand consultant for *Sesame Street*, the most widely viewed children's television series in the world, creating and implementing multiplatform brand marketing programs. This involved communicating and negotiating with people who essentially spoke different languages—curriculum researchers, consumer product managers, creative and production experts, marketing and media specialists, educational advisors, and publishing executives, among others. A heightened awareness of the importance of reaching and impacting these diverse audiences was critical to the success of our interactions and the implementation of multiplatform brand initiatives.

Periodically, I flew to Budapest, Hungary, and Stockholm, Sweden, where I worked with a British colleague as an advisory team to programming and marketing executives at recently privatized television networks. He and I developed and evaluated strategic brand plans for our clients. The cultural differences in behavior, thinking, assumptions, and values among my American, Hungarian, and Swedish clients and, of course, my British colleague, were both dramatic and subtle. The configuration of control and status-related issues, negotiation strategies, business and religious practices, and communication styles changed from situation to situation. Faced with cross-cultural uncertainties and ambiguities and the need to be effective interpersonally, I again resorted to my knowledge and skills in acting and improvisation to shift approaches and make behavioral adjustments. Aware of the need to adapt continuously to changing contexts and conditions, I learned as I went along.

Seeing Teaching and Learning through the Education Lens

This mode of improvisational, experiential learning is now central to my approach to coaching. From my business experiences, I discovered that adaptation to shifting cultural patterns requires cognitive and behavioral flexibility, analytical perception, and, often, suspension of judgment. I also gained a deeper understanding of my own cultural values and behavior by looking at contrasting cultural perspectives. Learning to appreciate and apply these understandings has been critical in establishing effective interpersonal relations in diverse cultural environments.

I had spent a great deal of time learning about learning, both in graduate school and through my own experiences. Eventually, I gravitated naturally towards professional development and corporate training assignments. My need to respond to new challenges and step outside my comfort zone had prepared me to adapt to new national and organizational cultures. That adaptability, in turn, helped me realize the importance of developing skills for learning to work in and with many cultures. I was drawn to intercultural education because it involves the process of learning how to learn; incorporating cognitive, behavioral, and affective dimensions of learning; and exploring multiple realities. Immersing myself in the study of facilitating cross-cultural programs, I became an insatiable reader of books on intercultural communication and cultural differences. In addition, I was mentored by several experienced cross-cultural consultants. These activities prepared me to conduct training programs for American executives relocating abroad and for executives from other cultures relocating to the United States.

I began to design and facilitate intercultural and business communication courses that incorporate acting principles and practices. One of the areas I currently focus on is facilitating learning experiences for executives and students that provide opportunities to acquire knowledge about diverse cultural orientations; practice adjusting their communication behavior; and reflect on their responses and openness to those who are culturally different.

Coaching Orientation

The use of actors' tools to try on new behaviors and practice responding to complex situations became central to my approach to coaching. Learning about learning is a continuous process for me. As a coach, I continually engage in open-ended situations that invite actions and responses in the present. Improvisation in life—as in art—is a practice of actively responding in real time to the needs of the moment. One action leads to the next and, moment by moment, the improvisation dynamically structures itself. This orientation is a result not only of my background and relevant influences, but also of my beliefs about coaching (see Figure 6.1).

BELIEFS

My beliefs about coaching have been shaped by my background and reflected in my actions. I believe there is a strong relationship between the arts and the cognitive process of inquiry. The artistic process of experimenting with word images, sound, and movement is a form of heuristic inquiry. It involves exploring new combinations of these elements, investigating how they interact with one another, what responses they evoke or don't evoke in others. Discovery, trial and error, observation, and evaluation are essential throughout.

From my perspective, both the arts and the sciences can help us understand the world in which we live. James Baldwin wrote, "The purpose of art is to lay bare the questions which have been hidden by the answers." The creative process is one way of understanding the world.

I believe the performance process involves accepting a high degree

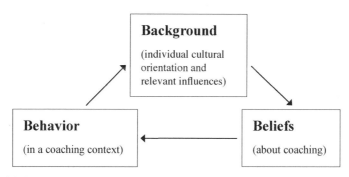

Figure 6.1 Coaching Orientation

of uncertainty, variability, and complexity. Responding to each new moment, to voices, and to relationships requires shifting directions as new things emerge. Based on my personal and professional experiences, engaging in and reflecting on carefully crafted arts-based activities can enhance cognitive and behavioral flexibility.

From my perspective, it is possible to strengthen one's physical and vocal presence, and to expand one's range of dynamic expressiveness. Connecting voice, movement, and feeling can result in authentic, persuasive communication. Strengthening the voice can result in more powerful and authoritative communication. Establishing and sustaining connection with one person at a time can result in impactful, compelling communication. Centering oneself, getting in a state of readiness, and focusing attention are practices that can be learned.

I believe that a theatre-based experiential learning approach can develop learners' awareness of choices and strengthen their ability to take creative action. When actors prepare for performance, they practice in rehearsal. It is interesting to note that the French word for "rehearsal" is *repetition*. (The Japanese refer to rehearsals as "keiko," meaning practice, training, and study; the Italians use the word "prova," meaning test or check, and the Germans refer to "proba," which means investigation.)

From my perspective, the use of theatre-based techniques is an effective way for people to practice engaging, exploring, and experimenting in open-ended situations. But keep in mind that these are my beliefs, shaped by my background. Your coaching model will be informed by the beliefs and values that guide your choices in a coaching context.

BEHAVIORS

As discussed, our beliefs influence our behaviors, particularly the way we coach. Performance Coaching is a theatre-based experiential learning approach that provides practice in engaging, exploring, and experimenting with action choices in open-ended situations. When people are faced with unfamiliar or uncertain situations, a dialogue between the individual's inner self and the outer world takes place. This particular kind of dialogue takes place in the context of each individual's attempts to understand and respond to or change a unique situation. It depends on three component processes: engaging in social interaction; exploring uncertainties; and experimenting with words and actions in the situation. Performance Coaching sessions are process oriented and outcome based; process precedes outcomes.

In my approach to coaching, I regard the dynamic interaction between individuals and the social environment as an ongoing dialogue.

There are many interdependent factors that influence the learning and change experience, such as history and culture. I recognize that multiple meanings take place in a network of relationships. These meanings are dependent on shared recognition and dialogue. Russian thinker Mikhail Bakhtin emphasized these dialogic relationships and the relational nature of meaning (1986). He regarded the people engaged in dialogue as "co-participants." In the Performance Coaching context, the dialogic relationship between the coach and the person or people being coached plays a central role.

From this dialogic perspective, "our ultimate act of authorship results in the text which we call our self" (Bakhtin 1986, 66). Adult learners are authors of their own responses. This is particularly true for people being coached who are engaged in open-ended situations. In this conceptualization of the ongoing dialogue between self and other, it is important for the people being coached to recognize their ability to shape situations by continually authoring responses that are meaningful and responsible. Performance Coaching calls attention to the dynamics of the improvisational learning process and its central importance in a complex world that is continually changing and becoming more interconnected.

Identifying and Selecting the Components of the Coaching Model

As I thought about the development of my coaching model, I realized I had carried out most of the reflective activities in Chapter 5, sometimes intentionally, sometimes in response to challenges. I had identified possible components and selected the essential components of my approach to coaching. Then, I was able to organize a model of my coaching practice. Gradually, my coaching model evolved.

I have documented the process I went through to develop a personalized coaching model in order to provide a detailed case example. Your coaching model will reflect your experiences and strengths, but the stages of coaching model development will be similar to those discussed throughout this book. Figure 6.2 contains a summary of the stages of coaching model development.

As I carried out the stages of action and reflection on my coaching practice, I became much more intentional about the process orientation and structure of my coaching sessions.

Process Orientation of Performance Coaching Sessions

Three major processes constitute the learning experience in Performance Coaching situations: engaging in social interaction, exploring

Identification and selection of your model components

- Review reflective activities and questions for reflection
- Identify possible components for your coaching model
- Select the essential components of your model

Organization of your model components

- Group and sequence the essential components
- Represent your organizing framework visually or verbally

Application of your coaching model

- Determine situations that will be served by your particular approach to coaching
- Build your practice or provide highly effective coaching for the people you manage

Reflection on your coaching process and practice

- Use your model as a tool for learning—reflect on your coaching interactions
- Continue to develop your approach—identify and commit to self-development action plans

Figure 6.2 Coaching Model Development Process

uncertainties, and experimenting with words and actions in the situation.

1. *Engaging:* The first process focuses on engaging in interaction. It involves adaptive responses for seeking clarity about a situation, and conscious action choices that express personal beliefs. The search for clarity requires connecting with others and engaging in meaningful dialogue. It calls for an external focus and involves the building of relationships with others through authentic connection. People who can respond to open-ended situations by taking creative actions that express their beliefs and shape situations become meaning makers, authors of their experiences.

2. *Exploring:* The second process involves exploring uncertainties and recognizing one's strengths. In this process, the person being coached explores and increases awareness of self and others in the social environment. Facing new or uncertain situations can result in an expanded awareness of one's own strengths, and of personal and cultural sameness and difference from others. Acceptance and understanding of these insights not only enhances self-awareness, but can enhance

the effectiveness of interpersonal relations and intercultural communication.

3. *Experimenting:* The third process includes experimenting in the situation. It involves a spirit of inquiry, along with intention and commitment. Special emphasis is placed here on the experience of learning by participating. The person being coached invents and tests strategies in changing situations, then experiments with purposeful action in response to the meanings found in the particular moment and the particular context. The person's ability to respond to situations with inquiry, staying in the moment and not jumping to conclusions, is an important consideration. Useful responses include investigation through observing, listening, and attending to the details of the moment before testing strategies of action. Two other factors drive purposeful action: the learners' intention in the situation, i.e. their attempt to achieve particular goals, and their commitment to staying adaptive to changes in context and response.

Structure of Performance Coaching Sessions

Performance Coaching is a method for assisting learners in making choices and taking action in interpersonal situations that are unique and complex. It provides an environment for the people being coached to practice interpersonal communication skills and reflect on their experiences. Goals vary from individual to individual, but, overall, the desired outcomes of Performance Coaching sessions are to empower people by strengthening presence and relationship building skills, and by developing trust and confidence in their own abilities to communicate effectively.

As I thought about my coaching interactions and ways to move people toward performing more competently in interpersonal situations, I realized that four phases are essential. Each Performance Coaching session has four phases:

Phase 1: Stepping into new situations in a safe environment
Phase 2: Investigating the situation and responding to others
Phase 3: Making creative action choices and taking intentional action
Phase 4: Giving and receiving feedback and support

Phase 1: Stepping into New Situations in a Safe Environment

A theatre-based experiential learning approach provides the people being coached with opportunities to work on their goals in a judgment-free environment, where failure is impossible and risk is essential. Every Performance Coaching session begins with a conversation, which, in fact, is a collective verbal improvisation. It creates and establishes safety, trust, and openness. The coach pays close attention to the physical, psychological, and artistic conditions that contribute and undermine a sense of safety. It is vitally important to create a sense of safety to support open engagement with situations of uncertainty. The opening conversation also clarifies the purpose for the coaching session and demonstrates acceptance, support, and positive regard for each individual.

Following the opening conversation, the coach suggests physical warm-ups, along with the most basic level of acting exercises (e.g. centering or focusing exercises) that can be used to enhance learning. Preparation and permission to try out new actions and responses in a safe environment frees the people being coached from relying on their usual repertoire of behaviors. Not only does this allow a natural curiosity, it encourages the people being coached to move beyond the safe and familiar.

Phase 2: Investigating the Situation and Responding to Others

In theatre-based experiences, the ability to "read" a situation while it is happening is essential. This ability can be developed through practice in observing, listening, and making adaptive responses to constantly shifting circumstances. During this phase of Performance Coaching, the people being coached do a variety of improvisational theatre-based activities; for example, listening to understand the ideas and concerns of others, then responding in ways that inspire and motivate them to take particular actions. These activities are an effective way to enhance the ability to take in large amounts of information, a crucial competence when sizing up and responding to new and unique situations.

Improvisational theatre-based activities require mental agility and sensory acuity, as well as the ability to accept and build on ideas. Through improvising, people in coaching sessions learn to pay careful attention to verbal and non-verbal cues, moving quickly from one idea to the next, and adjusting to new information as it becomes available. They learn the importance of being in a state of centered readiness, as well as the need for openness and responsiveness. They not only expand their repertoire of responses but also develop greater focus, flexibility, and confidence in their ability to think quickly on their feet.

Continued practice leads to heightened awareness and increased capacity to take in different types of information. As they practice, they also learn to respond appropriately and effectively with words and actions in a variety of given circumstances.

Phase 3: Making Creative Action Choices and Taking Intentional Action
Theatre-based learning involves seeing available options and shaping uncertainties and ambiguities. This means thinking in terms of possibilities within the given circumstances and making action choices. During this phase of Performance Coaching, the people being coached practice making choices and explore a multiplicity of possible actions and responses to those actions. They consider the *who, what, when,* and *where* of the given circumstances, and the *why* of their actions—their intention or purpose. They are involved in theatre-based activities that require them to choose and execute actions to achieve their intentions and overcome obstacles. For example, in one activity a business leader constructs a memorable narrative that illustrates a complex principle or introduces a new vision to various global teams.

By engaging in theatre-based experiences, people in the coaching session focus on the process of identifying their intentions, making choices, and taking actions. It is important for them to clearly articulate their own intentions and be aware of possible obstacles in the way of attaining them. Equally important is their identification of changes in the given circumstances and their ability to adapt their actions expediently to the changing circumstances.

Phase 4: Giving and Receiving Feedback and Support
In a theatre-based practice, learners observe and respond to others. They also give and receive authentic, constructive, balanced feedback. This feedback either reinforces desired behaviors or redirects undesired behavior. It acknowledges and informs people about the impact of their actions on others or on business outcomes. Awareness of self and other is fostered and increased in the relational context of Performance Coaching sessions. People experience support and challenge. They are not alone in the process and move gradually toward experiencing themselves as part of a dialogue with others, supporting and contributing their voices to a collective experience. Most important, the coaching process helps people gain confidence in challenging themselves to continue learning, to build better relationships, to communicate more effectively, and to improve their performance in an organizational context.

INDIVIDUAL CULTURAL ORIENTATION

Unique Set of Experiences	Unique Set of Perspectives
• **Participation** Meaningful personal and professional experiences	• **Cultural Background** Group memberships that influence your sense of identity, e.g. discipline, industry, education, organization, geography, family of origin
• **Social Connections** Key contacts who influence your ways of thinking and acting	• **Communication Behavior Norms** Forms and norms of communication behavior
• **Interests and Expertise** Major interests and areas of expertise	• **Core Values and Beliefs** Guiding principles, core values, and beliefs
• **Contexts** Settings in which your communication takes place	• **Individual Traits** Personal style, qualities, competencies, strengths

COACHING ORIENTATION

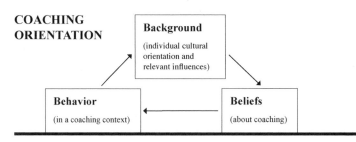

Background
(individual cultural orientation and relevant influences)

Behavior
(in a coaching context)

Beliefs
(about coaching)

DEVELOPMENT PROCESS

Identification and selection of your model components

- Review reflective activities and questions for reflection.
- Identify possible components for your coaching model.
- Select the essential components of your model.

Organization of your model components

- Group and sequence the essential components.
- Represent your organizing framework visually or verbally.

Application of your coaching model

- Determine situations that will be served by your particular approach to coaching.
- Build your practice or provide highly effective coaching for the people you manage.

Reflection on your coaching process and practice

- Use your model as a tool for learning—reflect on your coaching interactions.
- Continue to develop your approach—identify and commit to self-development action plans.

Figure 6.3 Development of a Coaching Model

SUMMARY

Performance Coaching is one example of a coaching model. This chapter has described the evolution of this model to demonstrate how one coach used the guidelines in this book to develop a personalized coaching model. Your approach to coaching will arise from your own individual perspectives, skills, knowledge, and experiences. Your cultural orientation will influence your coaching orientation. Figure 6.3 shows the factors that inform your coaching orientation and the stages of coaching model development.

Once you have developed your model, you can focus on applying it in organizational settings. You also can use your model as a personalized tool for reflecting on your coaching process and practice, facilitating your learning, and for improvement of your coaching effectiveness.

Your model of coaching can be applied to a wide variety of situations. In the next chapter, specific business and academic applications of the Performance Coaching Model are discussed. The Performance Coaching Model is used as a case example of how a coaching model can be applied in different contexts.

7

HOW THE PERFORMANCE COACHING
MODEL IS APPLIED

This chapter describes various applications of one coaching model. The descriptions are intended to illustrate the many ways one coaching model can be applied in organizational settings. They are also meant to stimulate your thinking about how you can apply your own model. The chapter begins with examples of applications of the author's Performance Coaching approach in business education, faculty development, leadership development, speaker development, and development of the coach. It ends with some practical suggestions for working with your own personalized coaching model.

PERFORMANCE COACHING IN BUSINESS EDUCATION

At one of the premier business schools in the United States, a new class of more than 400 graduate students enters a two-year MBA program each year. Every student in this program is required to attend a coaching session during his or her first semester in the program. Each coaching session, attended by eight students, lasts three hours and is based on the Performance Coaching Model discussed in the preceding chapter. The session begins with a group discussion to engage all the participants. They identify their needs, interests, concerns, and goals related to ways they present themselves and to their interpersonal effectiveness. Based on the issues the students raise, specific acting techniques are practiced to strengthen communication and interpersonal skills. Students then apply the techniques in individual impromptu speeches with coaching during the session. This simple format focuses on and deepens each individual's strengths, reinforced by immediate constructive feedback from peers and the coach. Although there is a pre-set flow, each session is different from all others because of the dynamics of the group and the uniqueness of each individual participant.

The Performance Coaching approach readily lends itself to honest and frequently profound discussions of issues of concern to business students, including issues often not possible to discuss in larger group settings. The discussions may include power and presence, impression management, confidence, authenticity, cultural clashes, surprising feedback, behavioral flexibility, and strategies for accomplishing intended outcomes in business settings. When students are viewed with positive regard and listened to in a non-judgmental manner, they are emboldened to speak openly and honestly in front of their peers.

This coaching program offers first-year MBA students a safe environment to explore new behaviors, unleash their power, and learn about achieving a commanding presence. To accomplish this, theatre-based, participative techniques are combined with practice and individualized feedback to strengthen the ability to perform well in challenging interpersonal situations. Participants gain insights and practical tools that can be immediately applied. The session ends with each student committing to a particular action. These business school graduate students are very impressive in the ways that they rise to the challenge to improve their performance, using their natural instincts for success. It is an honor and a privilege for me to coach these MBA students.

In business education, Performance Coaching programs include stand-alone sessions; coaching sessions triggered by upcoming events, important meetings, presentations, or competitions; and coaching to fulfill the MBA program course requirement. The starting point in all cases comes from the people being coached. As their Performance Coach, my overall goal is to acknowledge and build on each individual's strengths and find the one or two key changes that will make a dramatic difference in his or her self-presentation and self-confidence. Feeling a sense of their own power and presence is invaluable for business students who are preparing to become future leaders.

PERFORMANCE COACHING MODEL IN PROFESSIONAL DEVELOPMENT

Faculty Development

The same graduate business school also used Performance Coaching with faculty. The head of a faculty development program invited a group of 15 senior faculty members and administrators to attend a half-day Performance Coaching session. The faculty had expressed interest in receiving coaching on their classroom performance to experience renewed energy and commitment to teaching. The coaching session began with a group discussion to introduce the concept of applying acting principles to teaching, and to uncover the participants' needs and goals through this approach. Following this preview, the participants were introduced to acting techniques that would help them connect better with their students and motivate classroom inter-action. They engaged in a variety of theatre-based experiential learning activities. These included: acting exercises to explore the relationship between actor and audience, and implications for teaching contexts; group improvisations to explore responding to given circumstances, and applications in classroom settings; and individual coaching and practice delivering monologues and speeches.

The enthusiasm of the faculty members and administrators, the depth of their curiosity about acting principles and techniques, and the seriousness with which they grappled with concepts and their application to the classroom exceeded my expectations. I learned from the feedback received after this and subsequent Performance Coach-ing sessions with faculty and administrators that they gained a new awareness of how to expand their range of dynamic expressiveness, engage audiences, and create an atmosphere of high energy in the classroom.

In addition to group sessions, Performance Coaching for individual faculty members has become one of the options in the school-wide faculty development program. Full-time professors, adjunct professors, and Ph.D.-student instructors can choose to receive coaching to improve their teaching effectiveness and to fulfill their obligation to participate in one of the offerings of the mandatory faculty develop-ment program. In these one-on-one Performance Coaching sessions, theatre-based techniques are selected for practice, based on the needs expressed by the person being coached. The intention for all faculty development coaching sessions is to provide support for enhancing teaching performance, and to create a self-generating and self-sustaining basis for continued learning.

Leadership Development

Another example of Performance Coaching for professional develop-ment took place in a major financial services company's training center in Tokyo. The coaching sessions, aimed at strengthening the leadership presence of executives in the global business environment, were a com-ponent of the corporate-wide leadership development program. The participating senior-level executives explored issues related to leadership rooted in partnership, vision and values, and leadership styles.

The coaching focused on increasing presence and credibility; building authentic connections with others; and gaining skills in communicating effectively during challenging situations. The theatre-based techniques ranged from physical and vocal presence exercises to action-response activities, improvised scenarios and presentations, storytelling activities, and feedback on delivery of scripted or impromptu speeches.

Through individual coaching, the executives discovered, enhanced, and strengthened their leadership abilities. The emphasis for some of the executives was on engaging other people to inspire and motivate them to action. For others, the emphasis was on establishing and maintaining a strong sense of presence or communicating authentically and persuasively in key business situations with internal and external audiences. All of the executives developed strategies for delivering effective business messages to their key constituents, including people from different cultural backgrounds. They gained a deeper understanding of their effect on the environment and improved their ability to communicate with and get results from diverse business audiences.

Speaker Development

Performance Coaching for speaker development starts at the ability level of the person being coached. The coaching focuses on building skills for content delivery, developing stronger relationships with audiences, and articulating and amplifying the unique qualities of each speaker. The speakers gain an expanded range of expression, as well as a broader and deeper impact on audiences. During some of the coaching sessions, audience members are brought in to listen to speeches and provide feedback on the impact the speaker has on them and their experience as audience members.

In addition to establishing and maintaining a relationship with the audience, participants in these coaching sessions may focus on the use of language to evoke images in the minds of the audience. They align their personal values with their speech and practice communicating those values to evoke the audience's own values. Often, the people being coached bring their own material, such as poems, excerpts from speeches, monologues from books or plays, or self-written pieces.

Performance Coaching for speakers again draws on the tools of actors, adapting them to business settings. In each coaching session, people explore new behaviors, take risks, make discoveries, and ultimately feel personal ownership of their learning. This approach to coaching starts with trusting the abilities of the people being coached and amplifying the strengths they already have. It then expands and refines the speakers' natural abilities, encouraging them to bring their unique points of view to their professional and personal activities. Sessions generally follow the four-phase process of the Performance Coaching Model: *stepping into new situations in a safe environment; investigating the situation and responding to others; making creative action choices and taking intentional action; and giving and receiving feedback and support.* (See Chapter 6.)

Development of the Coach

Performance Coaching has also been applied to the development of people interested in becoming more effective in managing and developing others. Used with emerging and experienced professional coach practitioners, as well as with managers in organizations, the model can strengthen their capacity to work effectively with clients or employees. In this application, Performance Coaching offers learning opportunities for coaches, facilitators, consultants, trainers, and managers in international corporations and other organizations.

Coaches and other professionals who facilitate learning and development are introduced to advanced theatre-based techniques for engaging in interactions that motivate their clients or employees to improve their performance. The participants identify verbal, vocal, and non-verbal patterns of behavior, then master strategies for using this information to enhance their coaching interactions and relationships. As a result of practicing coaching in a feedback-rich environment, they increase their confidence in their ability to achieve intended results through skillful coaching communication. At the end of the coaching engagement, people have acknowledged a sense of satisfaction in having made progress in many areas, including: improving their observation skills; working with challenging clients; understanding how to adjust physical and vocal behavior when working with people who are culturally different; and knowing how and when to use theatre-based techniques in a coaching context.

When coaches and others responsible for developing people in organizational contexts are participants in Performance Coaching, they learn to use a repertoire of theatre-based techniques in their coaching practice. These techniques also enlarge the coach's capacities to experience different points of view and empathize with others. Central to the Performance Coaching approach is a shift from concentration on self to concentration on the audience, whether a group or individual. For every coach, this is essential. To be effective, coaches must pay focused attention to the person being coached and create a relationship of mutual trust and respect.

Performance Coaching, particularly when applied to the development of coaching effectiveness, highlights the importance of understanding and respecting the unique world view and the distinct culture of the person being coached. It is useful to view each coaching experience as an intercultural interaction; in other words, assume difference rather than similarity. In practice sessions, coaches attend to their own verbal communication to make sure it is clear, concise, and free of colloquial or technical jargon. Equally important is attending to non-verbal communication, such as gestures and facial expressions that emphasize and reinforce verbal messages. Coaches also practice communication techniques such as paraphrasing to check that what they heard is what the person being coached intended to communicate.

The opportunity to work with coaches and others involved in professional development extends my own awareness of how to use theatre-based processes in coaching contexts. It allows me to use a vocabulary that comes from acting principles to articulate a paradigm of performing that enriches coaching in organizational settings. In addition, working with people who support others' efforts to change performance inspires me to continue expanding my thinking about the process and practice of coaching.

REFLECTIONS ON THE COACHING MODEL

After you have developed your coaching model, you can use it as a tool for reflection on your own coaching philosophy, core practices, and plans for improving coaching effectiveness. Some of my personal reflections follow as an example.

As I apply the Performance Coaching Model, I am aware of the importance of context. When people participate in a Performance Coaching session, they step out of their daily routines into a new context in which they can face reality and conceive of new ways to move beyond perceived limitations. To create the coaching environment as a location of possibility, there must be mutual trust and openness in the coaching relationship.

This begins by getting to know one another, often by the sharing of stories, goals, roles, and backgrounds. It is important to learn about the person being coached—their filters and needs, level of experience and skill development, as well as the impact of the organizational context on their behavior. Establishing trust and freedom of expression in the coaching context also involves explicitly discussing intentions; that is, making a commitment to the coaching partnership, agreeing to confidentiality, and telling the truth. In my view, it is this shared commitment that forms the foundation of a successful coaching relationship in which learning through exploration and experience becomes possible. Then, each Performance Coaching session can be contextualized in the experience and knowledge of the person being coached.

As I apply the Performance Coaching Model, I am aware that I have my own ways of making sense of the world. I continually capitalize on my background in theatre, international marketing, and education. I draw on my experiences as a theatre director, teacher of acting to non-actors, and consultant to business executives in a variety of organizational settings. Throughout this book, as you considered the questions and worked through the activities, you have also heightened your awareness of your own sources.

I find it energizing to share the tools and techniques of improvisational theatre, and to use the vocabulary of movement and voice that I've learned and developed over the years, with businesspeople in a variety of learning contexts. My preferred way to learn about people is to observe behavior, to listen to what is and is not being said, and to focus attention on their strengths, resources, and resiliency. In coaching sessions, I use the skills I first learned as an actor. Further developing and refining those skills and my approach to coaching is an ongoing process that revitalizes and reinvigorates me. Build what energizes you into your model.

For many years, entering an empty theatre or empty space has been a stimulating and exciting experience for me because it seems filled with possibilities—communicative possibilities. The environment for my coaching sessions is essentially an empty room. For businesspeople, entering a Performance Coaching session in an empty space—a room with no tables and just enough chairs for the people in attendance—takes them out of their everyday work environment. It eliminates distractions and enables them to see things from new and multiple perspectives. In coaching sessions, the people being coached can move freely and explore new ways of using their bodies and voices to communicate authentically, congruently, and effectively. No props are needed. Their instrument is their body and voice, as it is in challenging interpersonal situations at work. They learn that they have what they need. Experiencing the coaching context as a location of possibilities is rich and rewarding for me, and, I hope, for the people being coached as well. Think about ways to align the environment you coach in with your coaching model.

As I apply the Performance Coaching Model, I am aware that coaching demands openness and flexibility. In the Performance Coaching approach, investigation is a central activity. Both the coach and the people being coached investigate immediate concerns, commitments, responses, priorities, and goals. To better understand the complexities, including individual cultural orientations and the salient factors that inform action choices, it is necessary for me to continue investigating throughout the coaching engagement. Then I can adjust my words and actions based on an understanding of how the people I coach see the world and what they care about. Performance Coaching demands flexibility—behavioral flexibility to match the styles of the people being coached in order to build rapport, and cognitive flexibility to adjust to their diverse needs and responses during coaching interactions. Given the complexities of individuals and the dynamic nature of Performance Coaching, it is important for me to remain open to new information that reveals itself and to communicate that openness to the people I coach.

Years ago, a gifted mentor coach gave me some valuable advice before my first coaching session with a senior executive at a consulting firm. She suggested I stay attentive to the clients, and remember that they would let me know what I need to do and what they want to do next. She reminded me that if I need more information, I can always ask more questions. Most important, she reminded me that I can give them time and give myself time. "Just encourage it forward." I appreciated her advice about staying open and flexible, focused on the person who is being coached—listen, observe, follow their lead, and build on their ideas to achieve the desired outcomes of the coaching engagement.

As I apply the Performance Coaching Model, I am aware of what my coaching approach does, and does not, offer. One value of Performance Coaching is its ability to help people become more aware of how they are perceived by other people and why they are perceived in that way. They learn new ways to interact, communicate and influence others, and to improve their overall performance at work. I see my role as that of a supportive partner, creating conditions and a context for the generation of new meanings and possibilities. My goal of being in the best service of the client requires me to be fully present and to stay focused on both the whole and the details at the same time. I believe coaching relationships need to be based in trust, openness, and honesty, along with appreciation and shared commitment. In the short term, I aim to support clients as they strive to achieve their goals. In the long term, I aim to improve the clients' competence when dealing with situations as they arise. When my clients can observe their own performance and make whatever adjustments are necessary to achieve their intended outcomes without me, I consider that a success.

During Performance Coaching engagements, there is no 360-degree feedback collection but there are in-person interviews and conversations as needed with colleagues and other stakeholders of the clients. There are no phone sessions; all interactions are face-to-face. There is a focus on presence, audience connection, behavioral flexibility, range of expressiveness, and intentionality. The Performance Coaching process is transparent—explained up front, including maintenance of strict confidentiality regarding the content of the coaching sessions. I find that explicitly discussing with clients what Performance Coaching does, and does not, offer allows me to be authentic and confident as I engage in coaching interactions.

As I apply the Performance Coaching Model, I continually learn and develop as a coach. For me, learning is an ongoing process. It has no endings. Unstoppable, it changes as situations change. As a Performance Coach, I want to continually build my skills, enhance self-awareness, and find new ways of doing things for myself and for the people I coach. I use the coaching model to continue my self-development by incorporating regular reflection. I also integrate, adapt, and apply what I learn from various disciplines, other coaches, as well as the people I coach.

I continue to think about my approach to coaching, identifying ideas that resonate with me. I continue to articulate my coaching orientation, either through speaking or writing. I clarify and sharpen my concept of coaching, philosophy, style, preferred actions in a coaching context, and voice as a coach. I continue asking questions. "How can we know if we do not ask? Why should we ask if we are certain we know? All answers come out of the question. If we pay attention to our questions, we increase the power of mindful learning" (Langer 1997, 139). And I continue to examine what works well, notice what challenges I face, and consider possible actions I can take to overcome these challenges.

These are some of my reflections. Long after you have developed or refined your own coaching model, I hope you will also continue to reflect on your coaching practice—and build on your current and emerging strengths.

PRACTICAL SUGGESTIONS FOR APPLYING YOUR COACHING MODEL

Because continual learning has critical importance for coaching effectiveness, I offer some practical suggestions for working with your own coaching model:

- *Recognize the power of your choices.* After each session, reflect on the way you chose to begin and end your coaching inter-action. People remember the first and last thing that happens. Refer to your model as you reflect on the most effective ways to begin and end your coaching interactions.
- *Develop a system of note-taking.* Keep track of important points and problems that surface during each coaching interaction or immediately after. (If you choose to take notes during your coaching session, ask for permission to do so and explain your rationale to the person you are coaching.) After the coaching session, review your notes and refer to your own model as you reflect on highlights and problems that surfaced.
- *Reflect on each coaching interaction.* After each session, use your coaching model to reflect on the key elements of your process. Ask yourself what went well and how it might have gone better.
- *Challenge yourself.* As you reflect on your coaching model, consider challenges you can set for yourself as you work with each person you coach.
- *Pay attention to your state of mind after each coaching inter-action.* If you feel (or don't feel) energized, alert, and satisfied after each coaching session, consider why.
- *Make your coaching model a functional part of your coaching practice.* Use your model as a tool for continual learning, planning for improved effectiveness, and reflection on your coaching practice. Evaluate how your model applies to certain business audiences or particular coaching situations.
- *Keep your coaching model current.* Periodically talk about your model with another coach—someone who you respect—and ask for feedback. If, at any point, you choose to modify the key elements of your model, do so. After all, your coaching model is a personalized tool for your coaching development; you, and your practice, benefit by keeping it current.

SUMMARY

I have described briefly the applications of one coaching model. The purpose of these examples is to stimulate your thinking about how you can apply your own model in various organizational settings. I have included personal reflections on applying my model to encourage you to reflect on your own coaching philosophy, core practices, and plans for improving coaching effectiveness. In addition, I have suggested some ways you can work with your model.

In Part I of this book, we laid the foundation for developing a coaching model, including an introduction to the purpose of a model, highlights from theorists on how people learn and change, and guidelines derived from their theories to apply to your model development and coaching practice.

In Part II, we took a deeper dive into the coaching model, beginning with the functions and characteristics that models share, no matter how different their approaches. You then began the process of identifying and selecting components for your model or of refining your model, if you already have one. As a result of investing time in the Reflective Activities and exploring your responses to their questions, you heightened your awareness of ways to incorporate—with authenticity—your beliefs, preferred practices, and strengths into your coaching model.

In Part III, I demonstrated how one model evolved, using my own Performance Coaching Model as an example. I invite you to explore the suggested strategies for model development. Continue your learning by refining, applying, and reflecting on your own personalized coaching model. As you observe your own effectiveness in coaching interactions, you can make whatever adjustments you think are necessary to achieve your intended outcomes—and those of the people you coach. Enjoy the adventure!

REFERENCES

Adler, Peter S. 1998. Beyond Cultural Identity: Reflections on Multicultural-ism. In *Basic Concepts of Intercultural Communication: Selected Readings*, ed. Milton J. Bennett, 225–45. Yarmouth: Intercultural Press.

Argyris, Chris. 1990. *Overcoming Organizational Defenses: Facilitating Orga-nizational Learning*. New York: Prentice Hall.

Argyris, Chris, and Donald A. Schon. 1974. *Theory in Practice: Increasing Professional Effectiveness*. San Francisco: Jossey-Bass.

Bakhtin, Mikhail M. 1986. *Speech Genres and Other Late Essays*, ed. Caryl Emerson and Michael Holquist. Trans. Vern W. McGee. Austin, TX: University of Texas Press.

Barba, Eugenio. 1995. *Paper Canoe: A Guide to Theatre Anthropology*. Trans. Richard Fowler. London: Routledge.

Bellah, Robert N., Richard Madsen, William M. Sullivan, Ann Swidler, and Steven M. Tipton. 1985. *Habits of the Heart: Individualism and Commitment in American Life*. Berkeley, CA: University of California Press.

Brookfield, Stephen D. 1986. *Understanding and Facilitating Adult Learning: A Comprehensive Analysis of Principles and Effective Practices*. San Francisco: Jossey-Bass.

Colvin, Geoff. 2008. *Talent is Overrated: What Really Separates World-Class Performers from Everybody Else*. New York: Portfolio.

Crane, Thomas G., and Lerissa Patrick. 2001. *The Heart of Coaching: Using Transformational Coaching to Create a High-Performance Culture*. Rev. ed. San Diego, CA: FTA Press.

Dewey, John. 1938. *Experience and Education*. Repr., 1997. New York: Touchstone.

Fitzgerald, Catherine, and Jennifer Garvey Berger, eds. 2002. *Executive Coaching: Practices & Perspectives*. Palo Alto, CA: Davies-Black.

Freire, Paulo. 2000. *Pedagogy of the Oppressed*. Trans. Myra Bergman Ramos. 30th anniversary ed. New York: Continuum.

Gallwey, W. Timothy. 2001. *The Inner Game of Work*. New York: Random House.

Hall, Edward T. 1976. *Beyond Culture*. New York: Anchor Books/Doubleday.

Hall, Edward T., and Mildred Reed Hall. 1990. *Understanding Cultural Differences*. Yarmouth: Intercultural Press.

Hofstede, Geert H. 1980. *Culture's Consequences: International Differences in Work-Related Values*. Beverly Hills, CA: Sage Publications.

———. 1997. *Cultures and Organizations: Software of the Mind, Intercultural Cooperation and its Importance for Survival*. New York: McGraw-Hill.

Hunt, James M., and Joseph R. Weintraub. 2002. *The Coaching Manager: Developing Top Talent in Business*. Thousand Oaks, CA: Sage Publications.

Jameson, Daphne A. 2007. Reconceptualizing Cultural Identity and Its Role in Intercultural Business Communication. *Journal of Business Communication*, 44 (3): 199–235.

Kemp, Travis. 2006. An Adventure-Based Framework for Coaching. In *Evidence Based Coaching Handbook*, ed. Dianne R. Stober and Anthony M. Grant, 277–311. Hoboken, NJ: John Wiley & Sons.

Kinlaw, Dennis C. 1999. *Coaching for Commitment: Interpersonal Strategies for Obtaining Superior Performance from Individuals and Teams*. San Francisco: Jossey-Bass/Pfeiffer.

Kluckhohn, Florence R., and Fred L. Strodtbeck. 1961. *Variations in Value Orientations*. Evanston, IL: Row, Peterson.

Knowles, Malcolm S. 1970. *The Modern Practice of Adult Education: Andragogy versus Pedagogy*. New York: Association Press.

Knowles, Malcolm S., Elwood F. Holton III, and Richard A. Swanson. 1998. *The Adult Learner: The Definitive Classic in Adult Education and Human Resource Development*. 5th ed. Houston, TX: Gulf.

Kolb, David A. 1984. *Experiential Learning: Experience as the Source of Learning and Development*. Englewood Cliffs, NJ: Prentice Hall.

Langer, Ellen J. 1989. *Mindfulness*. Cambridge, MA: Da Capo Press.

———. 1997. *The Power of Mindful Learning*. Reading: Addison-Wesley.

Lave, Jean, and Etienne Wenger. 1991. *Situated Learning: Legitimate Peripheral Participation*. Cambridge: Cambridge University Press.

Lindeman, Eduard C. 1926. *The Meaning of Adult Education*. New York: New Republic.

Maslow, Abraham H., James Fadiman and Robert Frager. 1987. *Motivation and Personality*. 3rd ed. New York: Addison-Wesley.

Mezirow, Jack. 1991. *Transformative Dimensions of Adult Learning*. San Francisco: Jossey-Bass.

——— 2003. Transformative Learning as Discourse. *Journal of Transformative Education*, 1 (1): 58–63.

Mezirow, Jack and Associates. 2000. *Learning as Transformation: Critical Perspectives on a Theory in Progress*. San Francisco: Jossey-Bass.

O'Neill, Mary Beth. 2000. *Executive Coaching with Backbone and Heart: A Systems Approach to Engaging Leaders with Their Challenges.* San Francisco: Jossey-Bass.

Peltier, Bruce. 2001. *The Psychology of Executive Coaching: Theory and Application.* New York: Brunner-Routledge.

Postman, Neil, and Charles Weingartner. 1969. *Teaching as a Subversive Activity.* New York: Delacorte Press.

Renwick, George. 2006. Coaching Global Executives, Contributing to our Clients: Possible Ways and Roles. Presented at the Society of Intercultural Education, Training and Research Conference, November 1, in Albuquerque, New Mexico.

Rogers, Carl R. 1989. *The Carl Rogers Reader,* ed. Howard Kirschenbaum and Valerie Land Henderson. Boston, MA: Houghton Mifflin.

Rokeach, Milton. 1973. *The Nature of Human Values.* New York: Free Press.

Schein, Edgar H. 2004. *Organizational Culture and Leadership.* San Francisco: Jossey-Bass.

Schon, Donald A. 1983. *The Reflective Practitioner: How Professionals Think in Action.* New York: Basic Books.

——. 1987. *Educating the Reflective Practitioner: Toward a New Design for Teaching and Learning in the Professions.* San Francisco: Jossey-Bass.

Scoular, P. Anne. 2009. How Do You Pick a Coach? *Harvard Business Review,* 87 (1): 96.

Senge, Peter M., Art Kleiner, Charlotte Roberts, Richard B. Ross, and Bryan J. Smith. 1994. *The Fifth Discipline Fieldbook: Strategies and Tools for Building a Learning Organization.* New York: Currency/Doubleday.

Silsbee, Douglas K. 2004. *The Mindful Coach: Seven Roles for Helping People Grow.* Marshall: Ivy River Press.

Singer, Marshall R. 1998. *Perception & Identity in Intercultural Communication.* Abr. and rev. ed. Yarmouth: Intercultural Press.

Stewart, Edward C., and Milton J. Bennett. 1991. *American Cultural Patterns: A Cross-Cultural Perspective.* Rev. ed. Yarmouth: Intercultural Press.

Stober, Dianne R. and Anthony M. Grant, eds. 2006. *Evidence Based Coaching Handbook: Putting Best Practices to Work for Your Clients.* Hoboken, NJ: John Wiley & Sons.

Ting, Sharon, and Doug Riddle. 2006. A Framework for Leadership Development Coaching. In *The CCL Handbook of Coaching: A Guide for the Leader Coach,* ed. Sharon Ting and Peter Scisco, 34–62. San Francisco: Jossey-Bass.

Ting, Sharon, and Peter Scisco, eds. 2006. *The CCL Handbook of Coaching: A Guide for the Leader Coach.* San Francisco: Jossey-Bass.

Ting-Toomey, Stella. 1999. *Communicating Across Cultures.* New York: The Guilford Press.

Trompenaars, Fons, and Charles Hampden-Turner. 1998. *Riding the Waves of Culture: Understanding Cultural Diversity in Global Business.* 2nd ed. New York: McGraw-Hill.

Vygotsky, Lev S., and Michael Cole. 1978. *Mind in Society: Development of Higher Psychological Processes.* Cambridge, MA: Harvard University Press.

Whitmore, John. 2004. *Coaching for Performance: Growing People, Performance and Purpose.* 3rd ed. London: Nicholas Brealey.

Zeus, Perry, and Suzanne Skiffington. 2002. *The Coaching at Work Toolkit: A Complete Guide to Techniques and Practices.* Sydney: McGraw-Hill.

INDEX